The Bat and the Bishop

Robert W. Prichard

Illustrated by
Kate Parrent

MOREHOUSE PUBLISHING
Harrisburg, PA • Wilton, CT

Copyright © 1989 Robert W. Prichard

All rights reserved. No part of this publication may be reproduced, stored in retrieval system, or transmitted in any form or by any means, electronic, mechanical, photocopying, recording, or otherwise, without the prior permission of the copyright owner.

Morehouse Publishing
Harrisburg, Pennsylvania

Library of Congress Cataloging-in-Publication Data

Prichard, Robert W., 1949-
  The bat and the bishop/by Robert W. Prichard.
    p.   cm.
  ISBN 0-8192-1508-2
  1. Episcopal Church—History. 2. Church of England—History. 3. Anglican Communion—History. 4. Church history. I. Title.
BX5883.P75   1989   89-32719
283'.09—dc20   CIP

Printed in the United States of America
by
BSC LITHO
Harrisburg, PA

Contents

Introduction	vii
Cyprian of Carthage	1
The Celtic Church	4
Henry the Theologian	7
Thomas Bilney's Comfortable Words	9
The White Horse Inn	11
Martyred by Salt Fish	14
Cranmer on the Eucharist	16
The Book of Homilies	18
Lady Anne Bacon	21
Richard Hooker on Authority in the Church	23
William Perkins on the Conscience	25
The First Baptism in British Colonial America	27
Robert Hunt of Jamestown	29
American Vestries	32
The Church of Scotland	35
Thomas Bray	38
The Sad Story of Thoroughgood Moor	40
Before Bishop Seabury	42
Unsuccessful Social Satire	45
A New Name	47
The Ordination of Weems and Gantt	49
The Free African Society	53
Weems, the Moral Reformer	55
A Changing Episcopate	57
Episcopal Colleges	60
Allen Gardiner	63
Charlotte Temple	65
Giving the Clerk the Ax	67
A Letter to the Presiding Bishop	69
Reversing an Episcopal Election	71
Frontier Bishops	74

Holding the Reins of Revivalism 76
Kaiserswerth 78
Bishop Kemper's Plea................................... 80
Dr. Alexander Crummell 82
The Renewal Theology of William Meade 84
Thomas Gallaudet 86
Jeptha's Vow 89
St. Andrew's Infirmary 92
The Bat and the Bishop 94
Enmegahbowh 96
The Ecclesiastical Career of John Henry Hopkins 98
McIlvaine Preserves the Church 100
Oakerhater and Alice Pendleton........................103
The United Thank Offering.............................105
Huntington's Quadrilateral 107
The Proposed Book and the Book Annexed 110
Neve's Dream..113
"Racial" Bishops and Archdeacons.....................115
Disappearing Balconies.................................118
Much Beloved Daughter................................120
The Death and Burial of Canon XV 123
Graduation Time in the 1940s..........................125
The Post-World War II Clergy Boom 127

Suggestions for Further Reading 129

Index 130

To Marcia, Daniel, and Joseph

Introduction

C.S. Lewis began his *Reflections on the Psalms* with an insightful introduction about the dangers of professional scholarship. Teachers, he suggested, were poorly equipped to answer questions from their pupils because they were so far removed from the problems that confronted newcomers to their fields of inquiry. Students would do better to seek the assistance of classmates because "the difficulty we want [them] to explain is one [they have] recently met." Teachers, in contrast, "met it so long ago that [they have] forgotten."

Lewis wrote about the problems confronting a student, but he could just as well have stated his proposition in terms of interests. Professional scholars often have lost interest in the issues that attracted them to their subject area in the first place. They move on to more complicated and more narrowly defined topics that do little to arouse the interest of new students in their field.

I hope that I have taken Lewis's warning seriously in the sketches that follow. I have tried to tell stories of the sort that delighted me when I first discovered history in grade school. Inevitably, my studies have drawn me on to the examination of more arcane issues—such as how did Anglican advocates of the Great Awakening handle covenant themes? But I have never entirely lost my love of good stories; I have found that their retelling is an important meeting point for the interested amateur and the professional academic.

People occasionally ask where I have come across the information that I have included in the following sketches. The answer is a simple one. The stories are the by-product of my teaching church history at Virginia Theological Seminary. They are the sort of nuggets that I uncover while preparing lectures, stories too good to forget but often inappropriate for the particular class or project on which I am working. Who could forget, for example, the sudden appearance of a bat that determined a bishop's election? But how does one find space for the story in an already overcrowded lecture on the impact of the Oxford movement on the nineteenth-century American Episcopal Church?

I began writing these pieces in 1982 when the *Virginia Episcopalian*, the monthly newspaper of the Episcopal Diocese of Virginia, agreed to publish a regular monthly church history column. The column on the Book of Homilies was later reprinted in the *Anglican Digest*. I have tried to select those columns with general interest. I have rearranged them in order to provide a more logical reading sequence.

Robert W. Prichard
Alexandria, Virginia
July 1989

Cyprian of Carthage

The *Book of Common Prayer's* calendar includes an entry on September 13 for Cyprian, bishop and martyr of Carthage. The name means little to most contemporary Episcopalians. The bishop, after all, died more than seventeen hundred years ago. Much of his writing survives, but nothing that he wrote has ever had the wide appeal of such works as Augustine of Hippo's *Confessions* or *City of God*. Despite Cyprian's limited reputation, however, at least some Episcopalians were not surprised by his presence on the calendar. He has always been something of a favorite among Episcopal apologists and church historians.

Part of the attraction has to do with the time and place in which Cyprian wrote. The bishop presided over the church of Carthage for a ten-year period in the middle of the third century. It was a difficult time for the church and for the bishop. His episcopate was bracketed by two periods of persecution: the Roman Emperor Decius's persecution, which reached North Africa soon after Cyprian's election to the episcopate in 248, and Emperor Valerian's persecution, during which the bishop died. Despite these persecutions, however, Cyprian was able to provide a detailed guidance to his diocese that has offered later Christians clues about the life of the early church. Prior to Cyprian, there was little concrete information on such basic questions as, At what age did Christian parents present their children for baptism? Cyprian provided some of the earliest clear evidence on this question.

When nineteenth-century Episcopalians found it necessary to defend the practice of infant baptism from the criticism of those denominations that limited the sacrament to adults, they turned to familiar biblical arguments: Jesus blessed the children in Mark 10, and Paul and Silas baptized a jailer's whole household in Acts 16. To go beyond this somewhat ambiguous evidence, however, they had to turn to Cyprian. Presiding Bishop John Henry Hopkins (1792-1868) followed this line of reasoning in his *Primitive Church*.

He cited Cyprian as his earliest evidence for the baptism of infants and for the appropriateness of baptism without immersion:

> The testimony of this ancient writer, on the subject of baptism by affusion, or sprinkling, instead of immersion, may be added here, in order to show its antiquity. . . .
> One extract more from this ancient writer, on the point of infant baptism, and I shall close this testimony.
> A certain presbyter, named Fidus, having desired to know whether the baptism of infants ought not to be delayed until the eighth day, according to the analogy of circumcision, a council of thirty-six bishops deliberated upon the subject, with Cyprian at their head, who returned for answer, that all infants should be baptized as soon after their birth as practicable, lest any suffer from the delay. (*The Primitive Church* [Burlington, Vermont: Vernon Harrington, 1836], pp. 54, 56)

Hopkins and other Episcopalians found Cyprian's testimony a valuable aid in understanding the practices of the early church.

From the time of the Reformation, Anglican and Episcopal scholars have noticed a second advantage to Cyprian's works. Not only did he provide evidence that was chronologically important, he also provided an alternative to traditions about church authority that originated in the city of Rome. Rome, like the city of Ephesus, claimed ties to the preaching of the disciple Peter. (The New Testament did not mention Peter's activity in either city, but the books of Acts and Galatians described his ministry in Jerusalem, Joppa, Caesarea, and Antioch.) By the end of the second century some bishops of Rome used the tradition about Peter (who was a leader among the disciples) to buttress their obvious leadership role as heads of the church in the empire's capital. Other churches in the western end of the empire should defer to Rome because the Roman church provided the same leadership that Peter had among the disciples. As the centuries passed, Rome repeated the argument with increasing assurance.

Anglican authors found, however, that the third-, fourth-, and fifth-century bishops of North Africa did not accept the Roman claim. Again Cyprian provided some of the earliest evidence. While the bishop of Carthage did not dispute the tradition that Peter preached in Rome, he rejected any implication that Peter ruled over the other disciples. English apologist John Jewel (1525-71) was one of many Anglicans to cite Cyprian in the Reformation debate about papal authority. Roman Catholics suggested that Christ gave special authority to Peter, which Peter then gave to the successive bishops of Rome. Jewel responded:

The old catholic fathers could never understand any such special privilege. St. Cyprian saith: . . . "The Lord, after his resurrection, gave unto his apostles like power. . . . the rest of the apostles were even the same that Peter was, endued with like fellowship, both of honour and of power." (*A Reply to Harding's Answer, The Works of John Jewel* [Cambridge: University Press, 1845], p. 360)

Jewel noted with glee that the bishop of Rome could not even lay sole claim to the title pope; Christians in the city of Rome had used the title also for Cyprian. "The priests and deacons of Rome write thus unto St. Cyprian the bishop of Carthage: *Cypriano papa*: 'Unto pope Cyprian' " (ibid.). Cyprian presented an alternative vision of the authority of the church—a fellowship of bishops rather than a hierarchy of authority in which one prelate presided over others—that Anglican apologists have found extremely attractive.

The Celtic Church

The religious setting in the British Isles is familiar to most: England has a deeply traditional national church; Ireland, a deeply traditional church in the Roman Catholic fold. The situation has been the same since the sixteenth century, yet if one looks earlier there was a period in which matters were precisely the reverse of what they are today. England had a Roman Catholic church, and Ireland a national church.

The period was an extended one, from 663 until 1152. England had been Christianized first. A Roman colony at the time of Christ, it was visited by Christian missionaries in the first or second century. The missionaries spread the faith quickly in the Roman areas, but it was not until the fourth or fifth century that they began to make inroads in the Celtic territories that had resisted Roman conquest. According to tradition, Patrick, a British Christian kidnapped by Irish slave traders, began a successful mission to Ireland around 430.

Pagan Angles and Saxons invaded the British Isles in the fifth century and soon suppressed Christianity in England. Celtic Christians in Ireland were, however, as resistant to the invasions of the Germans as they had been to those of Rome. They kept Christianity alive during the sixth and seventh centuries. The center of this continuing church was the monastery. It served as a base for education, art, and missionary activity. The abbot was the leader of the church, even when he was not the local bishop. Irish monasteries sent missionaries to Scotland, northern England, northern Europe, and even to Russia.

England was, however, the object of missionary attention from another direction as well. Roman missionaries would arrive at the very close of the sixth century.

The role of the Roman church had changed radically after the breakup of the Roman Empire in the fifth century. Prior to the decay of the empire, Christians throughout the world had gathered regularly in general councils. Bishops from larger cities or those with older churches had been accorded greater respect at the councils; they also had gradually acquired a supervisory role over neighboring bishops with smaller, less important churches. Yet no single bishop had exercised jurisdiction over the entire church, and many bishops (such as those in the British Isles) were independent of the bishops from the major centers. With the breakdown of the empire, communication between Christians in various parts of the world became more difficult, and Christians began to lose a sense of the shared leadership of the church.

The bishops of Rome brought Roman organizational ability to the more chaotic, postempire period. They divided neighboring areas of Europe into provinces and dioceses. Each diocese had a bishop who pledged obedience to the provincial bishop; each provincial bishop pledged obedience to the bishop of Rome. By the late sixth century, Roman bishops were ready to incorporate England in this hierarchical system. Encouraged by the marriage of Ethelbert (the monarch of a small Anglo-Saxon kingdom in southwestern England) to Bertha (a princess from a French kingdom that had already acknowledged the leadership of Rome), Bishop Gregory the Great of Rome sent a missionary delegation to England in 596. Augustine, the leader of the delegation, converted Ethelbert and established the rudiments of a provincial and diocesan system in southern England. Before his death, Augustine served as the first archbishop of Canterbury.

By the middle of the seventh century the competing Celtic and Roman missionaries succeeded in reintroducing most of England to the Christian faith. The question for many was no longer whether England was to be Christian but what form that Christianity was to take. Would the English preserve the monastic Christianity of the Celts or the hierarchical diocesan Christianity of Rome? A number of minor issues complicated the question. The Romans used a different calendar from the Celts and preached in a different language.

They demanded that clergy shave the crown of their heads and that those ordained by Celtic bishops be reordained.

In 663 at the Synod of Whitby, English Christians from Northumbria, including many converted by Celtic missionaries from the north, decided in favor of Rome. Other English kingdoms followed suit. For the next nine hundred years, England would be part of the Roman Catholic provincial system.

The Celtic Christians in Ireland (and in parts of Wales and Scotland) continued their independent life, however. As in the case of England, it would be the intervention of the French that would eventually bring Ireland into the Roman fold. In 1066 the Norman French, who were Roman Catholics, crossed the English Channel and conquered England. By the twelfth century they had moved into Ireland. In 1152 the Irish Christians at the Synod of Kells accepted the inevitable and pledged obedience to Rome.

Ironically, it has been English Christians who have kept alive the history of the Celtic church. English Reformers in the sixteenth century, looking for a precedent for an independent national church, took great joy in the Celtic history. The church calendar of the Episcopal Church today still witnesses to that interest. Among the names of Celtic Christians included in the calendar are Patrick; Columba (founder of a missionary community off the coast of Scotland); Aidan, Cuthert, Chad, and Hilda (Celtic Christians associated with the missionary community of Lindisfarne, from which northern England was Christianized); David (a Welsh bishop); and Willibrord (a Celtic missionary to Holland).

John T. McNeill's The Celtic Churches *(Chicago: University of Chicago Press, 1974) is one of the better books available about the Celtic Christians.*

Henry the Theologian

Henry VIII, the English monarch best remembered for his notable failure at monogamy, was for one brief period in his reign a theologian. Though his works during the period—1520 to 1523—were seen by others at the time as a simple refutation of the Reformation in Germany, they provided an important insight into the course of church affairs in England in the following two decades.

Before the death of his older brother left him heir to the throne, Henry had been preparing for the priesthood. Though his preliminary studies in theology were halted, they were not forgotten. When Martin Luther published *Babylonian Captivity* (1520), a stinging critique of the Roman Catholic sacramental system, Henry's ire was roused. With the help of Thomas More, he brought his theological skills to play and prepared a royal reply, *The Assertion of the Seven Sacraments*. This would in turn bring a reply from Luther and a response to Luther on Henry's behalf by More. By 1523, the debate halted.

Luther suggested in *Babylonian Captivity* that any sacrament necessarily involved two factors: a sign and a divine promise. Using this criterion, he argued that only two of the traditional seven ordinances of the church were properly called sacraments. These were baptism and the eucharist. The remaining five were not sacraments: penance, matrimony, ordination, confirmation, and extreme unction.

Henry attacked this treatment of the sacraments in a number of ways. His most consistent approach, however, was a social and moral one. Sacraments, he argued, were necessary to keep order in the realm. By their very existence, they taught Christians to live lawful lives. Without penance, his subjects would not do what was right and avoid those things that were wrong. Without marriage, they would not form stable relationships and raise families. Without confirmation, they would not teach the Christian faith to their children. Without ordination, they would not respect the clergy. By questioning the sacramental integrity of these rites, Luther was advocating social chaos.

Pope Leo X awarded Henry the title "Defender of the Faith" for his volume, but the pope should have examined the document more closely. Henry offered none of the traditional defences for the papacy—the doctrine of the two swords or the designation of Peter as the rock—but argued instead from custom. The papacy was justified by its long existence. Since the office had been around so long, the people must have consented to it. The rationale was, however, a flimsy one. An expression of popular discontent—such as that which Henry would engineer in the parliament in the 1530s—robbed the argument of its force.

In the two decades that would follow, Henry would remain remarkably consistent in his attitude toward the sacraments. Though his desire for a divorce from Catherine of Aragon would later lead him to turn from Thomas More and Archbishop of York Thomas Wolsey to seek advice from those more supportive of independence from Rome and more anxious for Reformation in England, he would retain his basic convictions about the sacraments. His 1539 Six Articles, with their restatement of the belief in the seven traditional sacraments, would shock many of the advocates of Reformation. Henry, however, was only holding to the position that he had stated in his debate with Luther. He might advocate nationalization of the church, dissolution of the monasteries, or the limited use of the English language in public worship, but he believed deeply that the seven sacraments preserved law and order in his realm. They were not to be questioned.

Thomas Bilney's Comfortable Words

In 1519 Thomas Bilney struggled with a spiritual crisis that would not only alter his life but also leave a permanent mark on the Christian church in England. Bilney was a theology student in his twenties at Trinity Hall, Cambridge. Like many late medieval Christians, he was deeply troubled by his own sinful nature. He desired a relationship with God yet was aware of the deep gulf between God and Creation created by human sin. Bilney pursued every avenue suggested by the medieval church to heal that breach.

Most Christians of the early fifteenth century went to confession only once a year; Bilney went much more frequently, hoping to use the discipline to purify himself of sin. In addition he fasted regularly, spent sleepless nights in church vigils, paid priests to celebrate the Mass on his behalf, purchased indulgences, and went on pilgrimages.

Bilney was not at all secretive about his plight. He corresponded with his bishop about his difficulties and asked the advice of others whom he respected. Yet none of them was able to offer him the comfort that he sought. In the end, it would be his own reading of Scripture that would release him from his search for assurance.

Dutch humanist Desiderius Erasmus spent a portion of his career at Cambridge. Though Bilney probably arrived in Cambridge after Erasmus's departure in 1514, Bilney knew of the scholar's work. Erasmus, deeply concerned with the place of Scripture in the life of the church and convinced that the Latin Vulgate translation obscured some of the meaning in the original text, published both a Greek text of the New Testament that was based upon manuscripts that he had culled from the monastic libraries of Europe and a new Latin New Testament. The second edition of the Latin New Testament appeared in 1519.

Thomas Bilney purchased a copy of Erasmus's new edition and began to study it carefully. Several years before, German Augustinian Martin Luther had found great comfort in the words of St. Paul's Epistle to the Romans. For Thomas Bilney, it would be the words of the pastoral epistles that offered hope. In particular it was St. Paul's affirmation in I Timothy 1 that Christ saved him even though he was "the foremost of sinners" that brought encouragement to Bilney. If Paul's persecution of Christians and his blasphemy against Christ were no bar to a relationship with God, then Bilney's personal unworthiness could be no obstacle either. Martyrologist John Foxe reported that Bilney afterwards referred to the passage in I Timothy as the "most sweet and comfortable sentence to [his] soul."

Bilney could not keep his discovery secret. He told many both in public and private of his experience. Christ, he told them, did not love men and women because they had been made holy by penance, fasting, indulgences, pilgrimages, and the purchase of memorial masses. Christ loved them in order to make them holy. Bilney shared his story first with individuals and then with a loose-knit group of faculty and students who gathered at the White Horse Inn.

Bilney was executed in 1531, and others whom he had influenced took up the cause of Reformation in England. He left, however, his permanent mark on the Church of England. We remember him today as the first English Protestant to die at the stake for advocacy of Reformation doctrine. We also have a reminder of Bilney's conversion built into the communion service. Thomas Cranmer, one of the young Cambridge students of the 1520s who was indirectly influenced by Bilney, imbedded the phrase that had triggered Bilney's conversion in the *Book of Common Prayer*. The phrase remains as a part of the Rite One communion service in the 1979 prayer book:

> This is a true saying, and worthy of all men to be received, that Christ Jesus came into the world to save sinners.

It had been in those words from I Timothy 1 that Thomas Bilney had found relief from his quest for self-justification. Through him they brought the Reformation to England.

The White Horse Inn

In the early decades of the sixteenth century, the White Horse Inn was a popular gathering place for Cambridge University students and teachers. Like many establishments in college towns, the White Horse served a double function: It offered food and drink for the body and a relaxed atmosphere in which patrons could turn their minds to major issues of the day. Thomas Bilney and the other regulars who gathered in the 1520s liked to discuss one issue—the current religious situation—more than any other. They shared both their own experiences and news of a young German Augustinian monk named Martin Luther. Indeed, discussion turned to events in Germany so frequently that others in the community began to call the White Horse "little Germany."

In 1517, Luther had posted ninety-five propositions for debate on the door of the church in Wittenberg. Luther was not given the formal opportunity to debate the propositions, most of which were critical of selling indulgences (special exemptions from acts of penance for the living and from time in purgatory for the dead, which were sold by the church in order to raise funds). But the superiors of his order did allow him to speak at a gathering of Augustinians in Heidelberg in the following year. Luther used the occasion to expound his "theology of the cross." Luther, drawing on themes from St. Paul and St. Augustine, taught that even the most diligent Christians would never be righteous before God. He urged others to recognize the inability and abandon any attempt to impress God with their works. They should simply admit their sinfulness and accept the total forgiveness given to them by Christ's death on the cross. Good works were done, not to earn, but to celebrate the love of God. "The righteous [person]," Luther argued at Heidelberg "is not the [one] who does very much in the way of good works, but . . . who apart from any works very much believes in Christ. . . . The law says, 'Do this,' but it is never done. Grace says, 'Believe in Him,' and everything is already done."

As the patrons of the White Horse knew, Luther was not only a skillful debater but also an effective writer. While a friendly Prince Frederick the Wise protected him from arrest for heresy, he began to produce numerous books and pamphlets calling for the thorough reform of the church in Europe. Many of the students and faculty members who gathered at the White Horse saw Luther's works firsthand, for by 1520 English merchants were smuggling a steady stream of them into England.

The higher authorities in England were not enthusiastic about the influence of the young German monk. Government agents began to seize and burn his books in 1520. And in the following year, King Henry VIII issued a refutation of Luther's sacramental theology (as discussed in chapter 3).

The Cambridge scholars who gathered at the White Horse responded to Luther's works in a very different way. They liked what they read. It corresponded with the ideas and experiences they themselves had had. They envisioned changes that could be made in their own nation's church. It is difficult to know with certainty all of the names of the Cambridge scholars who met at the inn, but it is clear that most of the first generation of English Reformers were in Cambridge during the years in which the White Horse discussions took place. The White Horse was the nursery of the Reformation in England.

This first generation of English Reformers paid dearly for their beliefs. Thomas Bilney was executed in 1531 for preaching against the doctrine of purgatory. John Frith was an unusually able theologian who fled to the continent and exchanged tracts with such Catholic loyalists as Thomas More. Frith returned to England in 1532, and he died at the stake in the following year. William Tyndale, whose translation of the Bible into English provided the basis for later officially sanctioned editions, was executed in Brussels in 1536. Robert Barnes, the Augustinian biblical scholar who assumed leadership of the White Horse discussions after the departure of Bilney, left England for Wittenburg but returned in 1535, while Henry VIII was contemplating a more Lutheran religious policy. Henry changed his mind again and had Barnes executed in 1540. Thomas Cranmer, later archbishop of Canterbury and author of the *Book of Common Prayer*, and Hugh Latimer, a popular preacher whom Henry would appoint bishop of Worcester, were also in Cambridge in the 1520s. Both would survive Henry's reign but die at the hands of his daughter Mary.

Tutor monarchs Henry VIII, Edward VI, and Elizabeth I carried out the legislative reform that separated the Church of England from Rome. The theological reform, however, began in other quarters: not in a royal palace, but in a Cambridge inn.

Martyred by Salt Fish

In 1528, English Cardinal Thomas Wolsey realized that he had made a serious mistake. The cardinal, a butcher's son who had risen rapidly through the church hierarchy through the patronage of Henry VIII, was well aware of his monarch's displeasure with the new ideas of German Reformer Martin Luther. As the archbishop of York and the papal legate in England, Wolsey was the primary spokesman for the Roman Catholic Church in England. It was his responsibility to battle against heterodox religious ideas. Wolsey, moreover, doubled as the chancellor for Henry's government. The cardinal shared the conviction of many early sixteenth-century English men and women that religious conformity was necessary to preserve the public order. Heretics were likely to be traitors. Had not the followers of John Wyclif marched with Sir John Oldcastle on London in 1414? The spread of Lutheran ideas had to be halted to save both the church and the state.

Wolsey's error in judgment was in part the result of his own pride. He had taken advantage of his authority as papal legate to dissolve the priory of St. Frideswide in Oxford and had used the resources of the priory to found an Oxford College. Naming the institution Cardinal College in his own honor, he sought to fill it with the best available scholars of the day. Unsatisfied with potential candidates already in Oxford, he had turned to Cambridge for faculty members.

As chance would have it, many of the bright young men of Cambridge of 1525 were members of the loose circle of friends of Thomas Bilney that gathered regularly at the White Horse Inn to discuss news of the Reformation in Germany. From this group Wolsey selected at least ten members of his faculty. Thus, Wolsey inadvertently staffed his college with advocates of the very Reformation ideas that his king was trying to suppress.

The Cambridge-Oxford rivalry undoubtedly contributed to the speed with which the leanings of the new college members were detected. By 1528, Wolsey knew that he had to take decisive action. He had the Cambridge men at Cardinal College detained. Several renounced their Reformation views and were released, but the majority of them did not prove so pliable. Wolsey had them imprisoned in the cellar of the college.

The cellar was a large cave that served as the food storage room for the college. It was stocked entirely with salt fish. The local authorities gave the prisoners no other food; for seven months, they had to subsist entirely on the fish. The diet and the poor sanitary condition of the cellar eventually took their toll. By August, four had died. Wolsey, fearing the harsh treatment of the college members might further publicize the irregularities at his college, arranged to have the surviving prisoners released.

Wolsey's actions—bringing the Cambridge men to Oxford and causing the death of four of them in the fish cellar—undoubtedly contributed to the spread of Reformation ideas in England. As Christians had learned in the early centuries, few things can spread the word about the faith with such power as the witness of martyrs. Later Anglicans would recall White Horse Inn leader Thomas Bilney as the first of the Cambridge Protestant martyrs to die at the stake for his faith. The four to die because of the fish cellar had less dramatic moments of death, but they were the first of the Cambridge Protestants to give up their lives for the Reformation.

Marcus Loane told the story of the first generation of English Reformers in detail in his Masters of the English Reformation *(London: Church Book Room Press, 1954) and* Pioneers of the Reformation in England *(London: Church Book Room Press, 1964).*

Cranmer on the Eucharist

In 1550, Archbishop of Canterbury Thomas Cranmer, the Tudor bishop whose hand shaped the English prayer books of 1549 and 1552, published his *True and Catholic Doctrine and Use of the Sacrament of the Lord's Supper*. In it he explained one of the central convictions that lay behind his liturgical efforts. Eucharistic theology, he felt, needed to be refocused. For too long, Cranmer feared, believers had seen the eucharist as a sacrament that had very little to do with the faith of the living.

For late medieval Christians, the eucharist was an important element in a form of spiritual plea bargaining. They believed that the souls of Christians who were not guilty of unrepented mortal sins went to purgatory on death, where they were purged of the stain of sin and prepared for Christ's coming at the last judgment. Since the process of purgation was to the medieval Christian an unpleasant affair—Dante's *Divine Comedy* depicted the envious in purgatory with their eyes sewn shut and the proud crushed under heavy stones—Christians sought ways to shorten the time in purgatory. Perhaps the most common method by which medieval Christians attempted to accomplish this goal was the memorial celebration of the eucharist. In the eucharist, they believed, the merits of Christ could be applied to a particular beneficiary, thereby shortening that person's period of purgation. Those who wished to pass quickly through purgatory hoped that surviving family members would pay priests to celebrate the eucharist in their memory. Those unwilling to rely upon the actions of others left endowments for the celebration of the eucharist in their wills.

Such celebrations of the eucharist became so common that average Christians came to regard them as normative. Christ was offered on the altar in order to hasten a departed soul along in purgatory. Laypersons witnessed such celebrations with great reverence—were they not witnessing Christ himself granting mercy to a deceased person—but they rarely received the communion themselves. The eucharist was for the dead and not for the living.

Cranmer was convinced that those who subscribed to this popular theology were deeply mistaken. Reading church fathers from before the tenth century, he became convinced that the primary role of the eucharist was to nurture the faith of the living. In his *True and Catholic Doctrine*, therefore, he repeatedly rejected the medieval idea of the distribution of merit. Those who taught that the celebrants at the eucharist "distributed[ed] by their masses the merits of Christ's passion" were contradicting "the manifest word of God" (1907 London edition, p. 33). He also rejected the doctrine of purgatory, for which he found no support in the Bible or the early church fathers. In addition, he cautioned laypersons who came to the eucharist to adore Christ's physical body in the elements. They were mistaken, said Cranmer, quoting the Nicene Creed, since Christ's physical body "sitteth at the right hand of His Father, and there shall remain until the last day, when he shall come to judge the quick and the dead" (p. 97).

In the place of a eucharist that was a memorial for the dead or an object of idolatry for the living, Cranmer wrote of a celebration that was intended by Christ to assure and strengthen the individual believer. Christ's death had been offered but once. In the eucharist, Christ came spiritually to the individual believers and assured them that his death ("one oblation . . . once offered," as Cranmer would point out in his eucharistic prayer) was for them. The believers were thereby strengthened and made new:

> As the sun corporally is ever in heaven, and no where else; and yet by his operation and virtue in the sun is here in earth, by whose influence and virtue all things in the world be corporally regenerated, increased, and grow to their perfect state; so likewise our Saviour Christ bodily and corporally is in heaven, sitting at the right hand of His Father, although spiritually he hath promised to be present with us upon earth unto the world's end. And whensoever two or three be gathered together in his name, he is there in the midst among them, by whose supernal grace all godly men be first by him spiritually regenerated, and after increase and grow to their spiritual perfection in God, spiritually by faith eating his flesh and drinking his blood, although the same corporally be in heaven, far distant from our sight. (p. 101)

For Cranmer, it was not what happened to the dead or even to the elements that was most important in the eucharist but what happened to the individual believer.

The Book of Homilies

In 1547, Thomas Cranmer and other members of the English Privy Council wrestled with a problem that troubled most European Christians of the day. They worried about the shortage of qualified preachers. Late medieval parish priests had been liturgical celebrants and pastors; they were not as a rule skillfull preachers. It would have been surprising if they had been. Most were not university graduates. Even those exceptions to the rule who had attended university were not necessarily qualified to preach in English; their university training had been primarily in the classical languages.

The Reformation had made the situation all the more critical. Beginning in the 1520s, younger university-educated clergy, particularly at Cambridge University, began to demand a thorough reform of the English church's hierarchy, liturgy, and doctrine. Henry VIII, always keenly aware of his own self-interest, was alternately hostile to and supportive of these Reformers. He appointed advocates of reform to positions in his royal government one day and sent Reformers to die at the stake for heresy on the next. The situation changed, however, with the death of Henry in 1547. Edward Seymour, the uncle and royal protector of Henry's nine-year-old son, Edward VI, placed the young monarch's government squarely on the side of the Reformers. The advisory Privy Council mapped a course of more thorough reform. The members of the council accepted Henry VIII's severing of hierarchical relationships with Rome and his dissolution of the monasteries. They added to it a new liturgy in the vernacular language (issued in 1549 and in a further revised form in 1552), a series of laws curtailing the use of imagery and ceremony, and a new theological statement (the Forty-two Articles of Religion of 1552, which Elizabeth later revised and reissued as the Thirty-nine Articles). Yet a problem persisted. How would the rank-and-file church members who lived outside of the intellectual and political centers of the nation learn of this theological reorientation? Certainly the laity would know something was afoot when the parish priest replaced the Latin missal with the *Book of Common Prayer* and took down the familiar saint's statue. But, if the priest could not preach, who would interpret for them the significance of the Reformation in the life of the church?

Thomas Cranmer offered one solution to the problem. If parish clergy could not construct sound doctrinal sermons for the benefit of their parishioners, perhaps they could read out sermons that had been written by others. King Henry, in the midst of one of his conservative swings, had issued a book of doctrine popularly referred to as the King's Book. Perhaps, suggested Cranmer, the young Edward and his Privy Council should issue a book of sermons that could serve as a replacement for the King's Book. Further, they could dictate the regular reading of the sermons in all the parishes in the realm.

The king and Privy Council agreed, and before the end of 1547 they authorized the publication and distribution of a collection of sermons, titled *Certain Sermons or Homilies*. The individual sermons were unsigned, so it is difficult for us today to know with certainty who wrote each line. Thomas Cranmer, Edward's archbishop of Canterbury, was, however, the primary architect of the book. He wrote portions, recruited others to assist, and tried to convince the more conservative bishops to accept the end product.

The book contained twelve sermons, each of which Cranmer had divided for ease of reading into three parts. The first exhorted parishioners to read the Bible. The second through the fourth spoke of human sin, the salvation offered in Christ, and Christian faith. The remaining eight dealt with specific moral issues (good works; love and charity; swearing and perjury; obedience; whoredom and adultery; and strife and contention), cautioned against falling from faith, and exhorted the believing Christian not to fear death. Thus the parish priest had a compact handbook of Reformed doctrine that could be used for thirty-six successive sermons.

After Edward's death, Queen Mary (1553-58) recalled the homilies as not in keeping with her conservative religious program. Elizabeth, however, reissued the book in 1563, adding to it a second volume containing an additional twenty-one sermons. The expanded volume continued to play an important part of the life of the Church of England well into the nineteenth century, though, as laity and clergy became more educated, they increasingly used the book for private, rather than public reading.

Eighteenth-century colonial Anglicans were familiar with the book. In the early nineteenth century, American Episcopalians debated whether or not to reedit the book in order to remove references to the English monarchy. In the end they decided the job was too large. Instead, they adopted the present addition to Article XXXV of the Thirty-nine Articles. The article recommends the homilies as containing "godly and wholesome Doctrine," but notes that "all references to the constitution and laws of England are considered as inapplicable to the circumstances of this Church." Theological seminaries used the homilies as a text for much of the nineteenth century, but by the twentieth century few Episcopalians were familiar with its important place in the English Reformation.

Lady Anne Bacon

In 1558, Queen Mary I of England died, leaving her half sister Elizabeth as her successor. Mary's five-year reign had been a difficult one for the English people. She had offended English nationalism by marrying a Spaniard and losing a war to the French. She had returned the Church of England to Roman obedience, executing 280 persons (including Archbishop Cranmer and bishops Hooper, Ferrar, Ridley, and Latimer) in the process. She had so frightened the large community of continental Christians who had taken refuge in England and those prominent English Protestants whom she did not jail that they all had fled to Switzerland and Germany.

Elizabeth understood that the stability of her reign depended on reaching a religious settlement in her nation. Convinced that neither the strident Roman Catholicism of Mary nor the energetic Reformed Protestantism of the latter portion of the reign of her half brother, Edward VI (1547-53), offered the possibility of a consensus, she sought to strike a middle ground. She allied herself with the first wave of English exiles who returned from the continent. Led by such men as Richard Cox and John Jewel, members of that first wave had used the *Book of Common Prayer* while in exile. Unlike a later group to return, they were not anxious to conform the English church to that which they had found in Geneva and other Reformed cities on the continent. Elizabeth appointed Cox, Jewel, and five other moderate exiles as bishops. Her parliament repealed Mary's religious legislation and reshaped the church in form slightly more conservative than the Edwardian Church of England.

The English church, however, still lacked a good and popular apology, one that explained the Elizabethan settlement in positive terms to the English people. Returning exile John Jewel had produced an apology in Latin, but it was of limited use for the large non-Latin-reading portion of the populace. Jewel's book, *An Apology of the Church of England*, ran counter to much of the literature from either Roman Catholics or continental Protestants. Jewel argued that it was unnecessary to set Scripture (the great Protestant authority) and tradition (the Catholic basis of authority) against one another. If one took the church of the early centuries as a norm for tradition, one would find little conflict between the two. The practices against which Protestants protested most loudly—the doctrines of purgatory, transubstantiation, and papal supremacy; and the practices of mandatory clerical celibacy, communion in one kind, and selling of indulgences—had not been standard elements in the church before the year 1000.

Archbishop of Canterbury Matthew Parker saw the value of Jewel's argument and authorized an English edition of the work. The translator, however, prepared an edition that was little suited to wide circulation. Parker was unsure what move to take next.

The solution to his problem came from an unexpected quarter. Lady Anne Bacon was one of four daughters of Edward VI's tutor. All were well educated. Lady Anne had particular gifts with languages. She had already demonstrated her skill by translating from Italian a number of sermons by the Reformer Bernardino Ochino. On her own initiative, she prepared an English edition of Jewel's apology.

Archbishop Parker was impressed by Lady Anne's efforts. Neither he nor Jewel made any correction in her translation. Parker authorized publication and added a laudatory preface to the book. "Madam," he wrote, "you have expressed an acceptable duty to the glory of God . . . honorably defended the good fame and estimation of your native tongue . . . and besides the honor ye have done to the kind of women . . . ye have done pleasure to the author of the Latin book in delivering him by your clear translation from the perils of ambiguous and doubtful constructions" (*An Apology of the Church of England*, ed. J.E. Booty [Charlottesville, VA: University Press of Virginia, 1963], p. 4).

Lady Anne had filled an important need by translating Jewel's Latin. Archbishop Parker urged other bishops to circulate the work, and at the beginning of the following century Archbishop Bancroft issued similar instructions. The translation became a classic statement of the English faith.

One of Lady Anne's children, Francis, would earn a place of respect, not only as a child of a leading translator, but also as a scholar in his own right.

Historian Roland Bainton included an essay on Lady Anne Bacon and her three sisters in his Women of the Reformation from Spain to Scandinavia *(Minneapolis, MN: Augsburg, 1977).*

Richard Hooker on Authority in the Church

In the 1590s, two of the best minds of the Anglican church were working on a common problem. The two were relatively young Elizabethan priests. One, Richard Hooker, served as the chaplain at the Inns of Court, the law school at which leading British attorneys and civil servants learned their profession. The second, William Perkins, was a member of the faculty at Cambridge University.

The problem that occupied their common attention was one of authority. As both were aware, the nationalization of the Church of England during Henry VIII's reign had created a theological power vacuum. It was one thing for English theologians and apologists to assert that bishops of Rome had, since the eleventh century, amassed hierarchical power for which there was no justification in Scripture or the early church. It was quite another thing to find an adequate replacement for that center of authority once England had rejected the claims of the papacy. Henry VIII and the English monarchs who followed him to the throne claimed the right to regulate the temporal possessions of the church and, at times, went further to claim a leading role in doctrine like that which the Emperor Constantine had played at the Council of Nicea. The behavior of Henry and his successors had made it evident, however, that there were problems with such a Constantinian model. If royal claims to leadership in the church were to be preserved, they would have to be carefully qualified.

The first generation of English Reformers had also discovered that there were problems with a flat assertion that Scripture constituted the primary authority in the church. During Edward VI's reign they found, for example, they could not even agree on how to interpret the New Testament's silence on the wearing of surplices. Did such a silence constitute an allowance or a prohibition of the practice?

Richard Hooker worked out his position on the question of authority in his *Of the Laws of Ecclesiastical Polity* (i.e., "On Church Laws"), a choice of a title that was, perhaps, not a surprising one for a chaplain to a law school. In the work, Hooker argued for three levels of authority. The first was Scripture, and the last was what he called the voice of the church ("that which the church by her ecclesiastical authority shall probably think and define to be true or good"), a source of authority on which Protestants of the sixteenth century looked with a great deal of suspicion. It was in the middle level of authority—reason—that Hooker made his greatest contribution. He argued that reason was itself a gift of God for the maintenance and support of human life, a part of an ascending scale of laws by which God ordered and governed the natural world. By reason, however, Hooker did not mean the result of individual thinking; he meant the process by which lawful authority reached decisions with the common consent of the governed.

With such an approach Hooker could provide the check against royal absolutism, which a Constantinian view of the English monarchy did not provide. The reforming policies of Edward VI and Elizabeth I's governments were reasonable and had therefore secured popular consent. Mary I's attempt to restore England to Roman Catholic obedience, in contrast, had not been reasonable. She was unable to gain popular consent and attempted to enforce her will on the nation with a reign of terror.

Hooker's argument seemed to have identified an important element in the life of the church. Later generations of Anglicans, even those who knew nothing of the English chaplain, would share Hooker's conviction that, after the word of Scripture, the consent of the people of God was a basic component in the proper exercise of the authority in the church. By itself the mere advocacy of a particular theological position by a person in authority did not constitute a final authority in the life of the church. Any truly reasonable exercise of authority would also have the consent of the people.

Hooker detailed the three sources of authority in V.8.ii of Ecclesiastical Polity. *[i.e. Book 5 Chapter 8 Section 2].*

William Perkins on the Conscience

Like his contemporary Richard Hooker, sixteenth-century Anglican theologian William Perkins wrestled with the question of authority. Perkins's own concerns led him, however, to approach the question from a slightly different direction from that taken by Hooker. Hooker called attention to the way in which three elements—Scripture, reason, and ecclesiastical authority—functioned as authorities in the church. Perkins sought to show the way in which two of the three—Scripture and reason—interacted.

In his *Golden Chain* and his *Discourse on Conscience* Perkins explained that human reason had been corrupted by sin, so that human reasoning was likely to lead to error and self-delusion. Nonetheless, Perkins argued that a remnant of the original righteousness that God had given to Adam and Eve before the Fall remained. This remnant was the conscience. Perkins believed that this conscience was weak by itself; it could be numbed or killed by persistent sin. Yet the same faculty could be shaped and strengthened by the reading of Scripture. (For Perkins, Scripture was the only element that had this power to "bind" or shape the conscience.) The conscience, so shaped and strengthened, then played a vital part in the human reason. Thus, Scripture and reason were complementary and interrelated sources of authority.

Perkins's understanding of the conscience provided a useful supplement to Hooker's understanding of authority in the church. A conscience informed by Scripture was central to reason. Reason not only told men and women to obey all lawful authority out of a recognition that God exercised authority through a descending series of laws but also because of St. Paul's admonition to "be subject to the governing authorities" (Rom. 13:1).

Richard Hooker's argument had clarified and shored up the claims to authority by the monarch and the bishops of the church. William Perkins's argument also had practical implications. Preaching had become something of a lost art during the late Middle Ages. Some bishops, for example, passed their entire episcopate without delivering a single sermon. The leaders of Edward and Elizabeth's church had done their best to remedy the situation by stressing the importance of preaching. Most parish clergy, however, read sermons from the prescribed Book of Homilies rather than preaching themselves. The number of clergy licensed to preach remained quite small. The effect of Perkins's argument was to stress the vital need for more preachers and to emphasize the central importance of the small group that was already fulfilling that function. Such preachers were the instructors of the conscience of the nation.

Later generations of Anglicans have not always shared the same concrete circumstances of William Perkins and Richard Hooker. From the accession of George I in 1714, English monarchs abandoned the active role in the governing of the church that Hooker was interested in defending. Anglicans outside of the British Isles live in churches that lack the close ties with the state that Perkins and Hooker presumed. Their interest in the basic sources of authority in the life of the church have a relevance for twentieth-century Anglicans, however, for they continue to look to Scripture, to reason informed by Scripture, and to ecclesiastical authority for guidance.

The First Baptism in British Colonial America

As many students of American history well know, the earliest baptism in British colonial America did not take place at Jamestown. The first British Christian to baptize in the New World had presided at a service in the Roanoke colony in August of 1587, a good twenty years before English settlers even reached the James River. What many do not recognize, however, is that Virginia Dare, celebrated as the first English child born in North America, was not the candidate at that initial baptismal service.

Virginia Dare was, to be sure, baptized at the Roanoke colony. Her parents, Eleanor and Ananias Dare, presented her for baptism on the first Sunday following her birth on August 18, 1587. The birth and baptism would stand in high relief in British colonial history, for the eventual failure of the Roanoke colony led the British to send only male colonists for the following thirty-two years. Virginia Dare was the first English offspring in the colonies; there would be no others until after the 1619 reversal of the male colonial policy.

Dare's birth and baptism were preceded, however, by an earlier event. Five days before Dare's birth, the members of the Roanoke colony had assembled to witness another baptism. The candidate at the service had been an adult.

Author and scientist Thomas Harriot deserves some of the credit for the event. During his stay in Roanoke in 1585, he had begun to visit Indian towns. As he later explained in his *A Brief and True Report of the New-Found Land of Virginia* (1588), "many times and in every town where [he] came, according as [he] was able, [he] made declaration of the contents of the Bible: that therein was contained the true and only God and His mighty works; that therein was contained the true doctrine of salvation through Christ; with many particularities of miracles and chief points of religion " (*The Elizabethan's America*, ed. Louis B. Wright [London: Edward Arnold, 1965], p. 131). Harriot returned to England to publicize the new colony, but those who continued the colonial effort followed Harriot's lead in preaching to the Native Americans with whom they came in contact.

The adult candidate at the August 13 baptism was one of those Native Americans who had learned of the Christian faith from the colonists. His name was Manteo. He was a local chief who proved a friend to the English colonists. The baptism was a cause of great thanksgiving. When John White, the governor of the colony and the grandfather of Virginia Dare, wrote an account of the events of 1587, he believed the event significant enough to relate it prior to the recounting of his own granddaughter's baptism. His brief words were the first written account of the celebration of a sacrament by an Anglican in the New World: "The thirteenth of August our savage Manteo, by the commandment of Sir Walter Raleigh, was christened in Roanoke and called Lord thereof and of Desamongueponke, in reward of his faithful service" (ibid., p. 136).

White returned to England at the end of August in order to seek additional supplies for the colony. He was prevented from returning to Roanoke, however, by the Spanish-English hostilities that culminated in the Spanish Armada (1588). When English ships finally returned to the area in 1590, they found no evidence of the colony. The colonial effort had failed, but White's pen had preserved for later generations the names of both Virginia Dare and Manteo.

Forward Movement Publications of Cincinnati, Ohio, has published an inexpensive volume titled Jamestown Commitment. *It is Owanah Anderson's account of the history of Native Americans within the Episcopal Church.*

Robert Hunt of Jamestown

In December of 1606, three ships sailed from Blackwall on the Thames, an English port east of London. The ships—the *Susan Constant*, the *Godspeed*, and the *Discovery*—carried approximately one hundred colonists for a new English settlement. Those colonists would name their settlement Jamestown, in recognition of the monarch who had just acceded to the English throne. It was to be the first permanent English colony in North America.

The hundred settlers faced considerable dangers. In addition to the hazards of transatlantic travel, they would face potentially unfriendly Native Americans, the possibility of Spanish attack, and the chance of exposure or starvation. They must have been aware that there had been no survivors of an earlier (1585-87) English attempt at colony-planting at Roanoke Island, North Carolina. Some of the colonists made a point of preparing wills before their departure.

Among the hundred colonists was one clergyman. His name was Robert Hunt. In some ways he was an unlikely member of the party. He was not a new ordinand with few ties to keep him in England. On the contrary, he was a settled member of the English ecclesiastical scene. Approximately thirty-eight years of age, he had earned both bachelor's and master's degrees at Magdalen College, Oxford. He had had twelve years of experience in ordained ministry in English parishes in Kent and Sussex. He was married and had several children.

It was not illusion about the safety of the expedition that led him to leave England with the three ships. He was as aware as any other of the dangers involved. He was one of those to prepare a will before departing. He left his wife and children in England but arranged with his bishop to allow them to continue to live in the rectory of the Sussex parish in which he had last served.

Nor does it seem likely that Hunt believed that his own health and stamina were sufficient to shield him from dangers that would menace others. Indeed, he was in ill health long before the expedition lost sight of England. According to fellow expedition member Captain John Smith, he had the opportunity of turning back but refused to do so.

To understand Hunt's motivation it is necessary to know something of his association with Richard Hakluyt (1552-1616). Hakluyt, like Hunt, was an Oxford graduate and an Anglican clergyman. He was fifteen years older than Hunt, however. At the point that Hunt was at Oxford, Hakluyt was already earning a name for himself as a geographer and a proponent of colonization. In the year in which Hunt entered Oxford (1588), for example, Hakluyt published a work titled *Principle Navigations*, a compilation of accounts of those who had explored North America. Ten years later Hakluyt printed an expanded three-volume collection of narratives. By 1606, Hakluyt was one of the principal promoters of the Jamestown expedition.

Hakluyt saw no conflict in his roles as colonizer and clergyman. To the contrary, he believed that the founding of a colony served a religious function. The peoples of North America had not yet heard the Christian gospel. English colonists could not only carve out territory for themselves; they could also bring the Christian faith to the Indians. The two enterprises were so closely linked that a failure in evangelization would result in a failure in colonization. In a 1582 work titled *Divers Voyages* he used this relationship to explain the failure of earlier English colonizing efforts: "If hetherto in our owne discoueries we had not beene led with a preposterous desire of seeking rather gaine then Gods glorie, I assure my self that our labours had taken farre better effecte. But we forgotte that Godlinesse is great riches, and that if we first seeke the kingdome of God all other things will be giuen vnto vs."

The other members of the mercantile company that managed the 1607 expedition chose Hakluyt as rector of the first parish to be established in the new colony. Recognizing both the importance of his role in publicizing the expedition to the English people and his command of geographical information needed for planning, the officers of the company did not object, however, when Hakluyt followed the frequent English custom of appointing a vicar to represent him in the parish to which he had been appointed.

Hakluyt could have chosen a young man without a college degree as his vicar; most clergy in the Church of England were not, at that point, university graduates. Yet he was convinced that an educated ministry was a vital part of the colonial enterprise; without it, colonists might not remember the religious aspect of their mission. Hakluyt invited, therefore, fellow Oxford graduate Hunt to serve as his vicar. The geographer must have shared his vision with Hunt in a persuasive way, for the younger man accepted the appointment.

When the ships sailed for Virginia, Hunt was on board. He served as a chaplain during the voyage over and, after the ships reached the site on which they would build Jamestown on May 13 of 1607, he began his parochial ministry. On the second Sunday after Pentecost, Hunt presided at the first Anglican celebration of the eucharist in the New World of which a clear record remains.

Hunt's ministry would prove to be a short one. He died the following winter. The pattern that Hakluyt had established with his appointment would continue, however. The English would send university-educated clergy to their new colony.

John F. Woolverton's Colonial Anglicanism in North America *(Wayne State Press, 1986) is a recent study of Anglicanism in America during the colonial period.*

American Vestries

Virginia colonists in the period after 1624 were faced with a problem. How were their parish clergy to be chosen? Before 1624 the answer had been clear. According to English church custom, the person who constructed a church building and provided lands for the support of its budget had the right to present to the bishop a candidate for the position of rector. If the bishop approved, the candidate took office; if the bishop disapproved, the patron presented another choice. The Virginia Company, which had created the New World colony in 1607, followed the English custom. It selected candidates for parish positions and presented them to the archbishop of Canterbury for approval.

In 1624, however, King James I dissolved the Virginia Company and placed the colony under direct royal control. James and his son Charles I, who followed him to the throne one year later, cited mismanagement by the Virginia Company as a justification for their action. In one important regard, however, they proved less effective governors than did the mercantile company. Neither of the Stuart kings made any provision for the continued appointment of colonial clergy. Indeed, Charles, who was married to a Roman Catholic queen, seemed uninterested or even hostile to the fortunes of the Anglican church in Virginia.

For a time the royal governor sought to assume the power of appointment previously exercised by the Virginia Company. The House of Burgesses, a representative body that was the forerunner to today's state legislature, had different ideas, however. Charles called the body into session in 1629 in the hope that it would grant him the right to levy a special tax on the tobacco trade. Once in session, the burgesses refused permission for the tax and moved quickly to the consideration of other issues, one of which was the appointment of parish clergy. In that session and in sessions in the following decade, the burgesses established a new pattern of clergy selection: Parish vestries were to select parish clergy and, in the absence of a resident bishop, to present the candidates to the governor for approval.

That colonial vestries acquired new authority in the seventeenth century would not have been a surprise to contemporary Anglicans. Indeed, in England itself, the institution of parish vestry was changing rapidly. Prior to the seventeenth century, the term *vestry* was used by English Christians to refer to annual congregational meetings. Such gatherings had been responsible, at least since the thirteenth century, for the care and upkeep of parish property. In 1598, however, the English parliament gave the vestries a new responsibility —the care of the poor. Seventeenth-century Anglicans, trying to take their new charge seriously, soon discovered that congregational meetings were too unwieldy to deal with the day-to-day necessities of the poor; congregational meetings began to elect smaller "select vestries" to carry out the responsibility. Indeed, as the seventeenth century progressed, the parliament added other, more civil functions, such as the care of the roads within the geographical bounds of the parish. The parliament never, however, gave the vestries the right of their Virginia counterparts; to this day they still do not choose their own rectors.

The burgesses' legislation provided for selection of parish clergy, but it did not solve another important quandary. Parish vestries did not have the financial resources to send interviewers to England to meet with potential candidates for rector. What were they to do if they inadvertently chose a rector who was unfit for the ordained ministry? According to the English custom of the day, an ordained person could not be removed by civil authority, even for the conviction of a crime. Only the bishop could remove a rector from office. A colonial rector that could avoid the notice of the bishop back in England could remain in office for life, regardless of behavior.

The legislature sought to deal with the matter by granting itself the right to remove unworthy clergy, but the vestries found a more pragmatic solution. The life tenure of a rector commenced with induction into office by the bishop or, in the case of the colony, by the governor. If a parish neglected to present a candidate for induction, that person could not claim life tenure; the vestry could dismiss the candidate at will. Many vestries delayed presentation to the governor, offering in its place a series of one-year contracts. In a time of royal indifference, the mechanism provided an important safeguard against unworthy clergy.

Other colonies did not all follow the Virginia example. In Maryland, for example, the legislature granted the colonial governor the right to appoint all parish clergy. In New England, the choice of clergy was practically in the hands of the English missionary society that supplemented clergy salaries. After the American Revolution, however, other states chose the Virginia, rather than the English pattern of clergy selection. Moreover, in 1804 the General Convention of the Episcopal Church departed from the English pattern in another significant way. It ruled that American clergy did not have life tenure in their parishes. Current canon law, however, does not grant the right of dismissal to vestries that colonial Virginians sought. The present rules represent a compromise between English tenure and colonial Virginia nonpresentation. Vestries may not dismiss their rectors. If they are, however, unhappy with parish clergy, they may appeal to the bishop, who has authority to decide whether a rector is to depart or remain.

Those interested in the colonial church in Virginia should see George McLaren Brydon's Virginia's Mother Church *(Richmond, VA: Historical Society, 1947). Borden W. Painter's "The Anglican Vestry in Colonial America" (Ph.D. diss., Yale University, 1965) tells the story of the development of colonial vestries in detail.*

The Church of Scotland

American visitors to Scotland are occasionally surprised to learn that the Church of Scotland is not part of the Anglican Communion. The Church of Ireland and the Church in Wales are both sister churches to the Church of England and members of the Anglican Communion. The Church of Scotland is, however, Presbyterian. To find the reason for this difference one must look back to the events of the sixteenth and seventeenth centuries.

The Tudors (Henry VII, Henry VIII, Edward VI, Mary I, and Elizabeth I) who occupied the English throne during the sixteenth century ruled England, Ireland, and portions of France. Scotland was, however, a separate nation with its own ruling family, the Stuarts. Thus, during the critical century of the Reformation, England and Scotland were independent, though neighboring states. The Protestant Reformers in the two countries agreed on major Reformation doctrines—the centrality of Scripture, the importance of worship in the language of the people, the belief in a justification by faith rather than works, and the rejection of indulgences and other elements of late medieval penitential theology—but they came to some very different conclusions about church order. In England, reforming bishops (such as Cranmer, Latimer, Ridley, Cox, and Jewel) envisioned a church that both retained apostolic succession and a fixed liturgy, and taught the content of the Reformation doctrine. Scottish Reformers did not agree. Their own experience would lead them to suspect that Reformed doctrine and catholic church order were incompatible.

In Scotland, as in the other nations of Europe, the national political situation influenced the progress of the Reformation. Scotland was a small nation with two large neighbors, England and France. Scottish monarchs, aware of their vulnerability, attempted to steer a middle course. They intermarried with the royal families of both England and France and alternatively aligned themselves with one nation and the other. By creating ties with both nations they hoped to avoid conquest by either. The policy was successful in preserving the nation, but it did have unforeseen consequences. The same policies that kept the French and English at bay encouraged divisions among the Scots themselves. On important issues the Scots divided into pro-English and pro-French parties. These divisions became particularly clear during the years in which Edward VI (1547-53) and Elizabeth I (1558-1603) occupied the English throne. These English monarchs and those Scots who sympathized with them supported the reform of the church. The occupants of the French throne and their allies in Scotland opposed the Reformation and arrested its advocates as heretics.

In 1559 and 1560, the pro-English Protestant party gained the upper hand in the Scottish parliament. Led by John Knox, a Scottish theologian who had spent time in exile in England and Switzerland, members of the party both limited French influence in their nation and established the Reformation. Guided by John Knox's favorable report about the church in Geneva, Switzerland, and aware of the French Catholic leanings of most of the Scottish bishops, the Scottish Protestants adopted legislation that differed from that proposed by fellow Protestants in England. Knox drafted an order of discipline that transferred the authority previously exercised by bishops to clerical and lay assemblies (presbyteries). He also prepared a general outline for worship.

Despite several setbacks, the Protestant party was able to preserve its position against the pro-French Catholic party led by Mary Stuart (Mary, Queen of Scots). In 1568, the Protestants drove Mary from Scotland, recognized her infant son James as king, and appointed her Protestant half-brother as regent. Mary fled to England, where Elizabeth I would eventually have her executed for her political intrigues.

Though the Scottish Protestants had relied upon English help to advance their own reform, they never saw themselves as simply duplicating English patterns. Their independence in religious matters would continue even after the two nations shared the same monarch. In 1603, Queen Elizabeth of England died, leaving no children or siblings to follow. The English parliament offered the throne to James Stuart of Scotland, who, because of the Scottish policy of royal intermarriage, was a cousin of Elizabeth. James, his son (Charles I), and grandsons (Charles II and James II) tried to bring Scottish church order more into line with the Church of England. James restored episcopacy, and his son introduced a Scottish *Book of Common Prayer*. Yet the Scots resisted these English additions to their Reformation and even launched an invasion of England, which touched off the English Civil War (1642-52), to prevent their implementation. At the century's end, monarchs William and Mary finally accepted the obvious and agreed to the Scottish church order. To this day the Church of Scotland has retained the presbyterian system that John Knox first introduced.

Thomas Bray

In 1689, Bishop Compton of London decided to take a new approach toward the American colonies. As bishop of the port city from which a major portion of English ships departed, Compton had, by custom but not by canon law, the responsibility for the oversight of British overseas missions. Taking this charge seriously, Compton began to appoint commissaries—bishop's representatives—for the American colonies.

One of Compton's early appointments was Thomas Bray, a priest in his thirties with a reputation for a quick mind. He had been a scholarship student at Oxford and had already attracted favorable notice for the publication of his *Catechetical Lectures*. In 1696, Compton appointed him commissary to Maryland.

Though originally managed by Roman Catholic proprietors, Maryland had become a royal colony in 1691. The first royal governor had persuaded the legislature to establish the Anglican Church. Learning of Compton's appointment of a commissary for Virginia, the governor had requested one for Maryland as well.

If one were to judge Bray on the basis of his assigned responsibility —the supervision of the clergy in Maryland—one would have to pronounce him a dismal failure. For the first three years of his term, Bray did not even leave England. By the time he arrived in Maryland in 1699, the sympathetic governor had been replaced by one less interested in the fortunes of the Church of England. Moreover, the Maryland legislature had repealed the financial provisions for the support of Anglican clergy.

Bray was able to convince the legislature to restore salaries for parish clergy. He so bothered members of the legislature, however, that they purposely included no provision for the support of a commissary. Unwilling or unable to accept a job as a parish clergyman, he soon ran out of money. Within three months of his arrival he sailed for England. He promised to return, but, despite the fact that he would live to the age of seventy-two, he never did so.

Three months were hardly long enough for Bray to become familiar with the colony and its clergy. Even where he did discover problems, he had little chance to remedy them. He learned, for example, of a clergyman with one wife in England and another in the colonies. He admonished the clergyman for his behavior, but returned to England before he was able to follow up his admonition with more concrete actions. He found, as had Bishop Compton, that it was difficult to discipline clergy when separated from them by the Atlantic Ocean.

Though Bray was a failure in the exercise of his primary responsibility, he was nonetheless one of the great figures in the history of Anglican missions. He compensated for the opportunities and abilities that he did not have with a remarkable clarity of vision and a masterful organizational skill. His brief contact with the colonies convinced him of the need for more, and more properly prepared, colonial clergy.

A skillful pamphleteer, Bray created interest in the colonial churches and with others founded two great agencies for mission: the Society for Promoting Christian Knowledge (SPCK) and the Society for the Propagation of the Gospel in Foreign Parts (SPG). The SPCK published Christian literature and provided for some thirty-nine lending libraries in the American colonies. The libraries helped to increase the educational level of the colonial clergy and laity, and they also served as effective tools for evangelism. The SPG paid salaries for colonial clergy. At the time of the American Revolution it supported a major portion of the colonial clergy in America. Since that time the organization had supported hundreds of clergy in all corners of the globe. Both organizations are still active today.

Bray is remembered on our church calendar each February 15 not for what he did not do—supervise the Maryland clergy—but for the important missionary societies that he founded.

The Sad Story of Thoroughgood Moor

When eighteenth-century colonial Anglicans gathered to discuss the relative wisdom or inadvisability of establishing a colonial episcopate, their conversation frequently turned to the story of Thoroughgood Moor. Advocates of a resident episcopate pointed to the downfall of Mr. Moor as a tragedy that a colonial bishop could have prevented.

Moor was a well-meaning clergyman who had come to the middle colonies to be a missionary to the Indians in western New York. He reached Albany in 1704 with the hope of moving to a nearby Mohawk community. European settlers opposed his plan, however; they argued that there were too few clergy ministering to their needs to spare any for Indian missions. Moor discovered that he was unable to alter the settlers' opinions. Learning that the Indians themselves were hesitant to accept his ministrations, he amended his plans. Perhaps, he reasoned, a ministry to the settlers was itself a necessary first step in the mission to the Indians. The colonists needed to set a better example of Christian life if they expected to interest Native Americans.

In accordance with his new understanding of his mission, Moor accepted a position in Burlington, New Jersey, becoming one of the first Anglican clergymen in that state. As he turned his attention from the evangelization of the Indians to that of the colonists, he became further convinced that the morality of the colonists was in need of serious reform. He was particularly concerned about the example set by the royal representatives. Lord Cornbury, governor of both New York and New Jersey, was a transvestite. The governor did not keep his behavior secret; indeed, he dressed in women's clothing and paraded around the city fortifications of New York, apparently for the benefit of the British soldiers stationed there. The behavior of Cornbury's lieutenant governor in Burlington was hardly more exemplary; he had a reputation for intemperance and profanity.

The rubrics of the *Book of Common Prayer* (1662) directed clergy to advise an "open and notorious evil liver . . . [to] presume not to come to the Lord's Table, until he hath openly declared . . . to have truly repented and amended his former naughty life." Taking the injunction to heart, Moor advised the lieutenant governor to reform or be excluded from the communion table. Moreover, Moor let it be known that he would do the same to the governor, were the governor to appear in his congregation. Lord Cornbury, who did not take such actions lightly, had Moor arrested and imprisoned.

The charges that Cornbury finally leveled against Moor—that he had celebrated the eucharist too often—would not have stood up in English courts. With the support of the bishop, who could often be counted upon to take the clergyman's side in such a dispute, and canon law, which gave a clergy life tenure in a parish, an English cleric in similar circumstances would soon have been freed. As Moor was soon to learn, however, colonial clergy could count on no such support. English canon law had no legal status in New Jersey, and the bishop of London, the prelate with nominal oversight for the colonies, was too far distant to be of any particular assistance. Moor remained in jail.

In September of 1707, fellow Anglican clergyman John Brooke helped Moor escape. Fearing Lord Cornbury, the two made their way to New England. They were offered parish positions by Massachusetts Anglicans but refused them, believing that their only safety was to be found in England. They booked passage on a return ship to England and made plans for presenting their complaints against Cornbury. The furious colonial governor learned of their departure and began a letter writing campaign against them. The protests by the governor proved unnecessary, however. The unfortunate Mr. Moor and Mr. Brooke both drowned before they reached England.

The frequent appeals to the history were decisive in convincing many Anglicans of the advisability of establishing a colonial episcopate. A resident bishop, many argued, would have come to Thoroughgood Moor's defense. Such a bishop could have prevented his long imprisonment and made a trip to England unnecessary. Such advocates of an episcopacy would have to wait, however. It would not be until 1784 that the first undisputed resident bishop exercised jurisdiction.

Before Bishop Seabury

The calendar of the American *Book of Common Prayer* designates November 14 as the commemoration of the 1784 consecration of Samuel Seabury of Connecticut. Seabury, the caption next to his name in the prayer book entry notes, was the "first American bishop." In many ways the caption is correct. Seabury was the first Episcopalian sent by a body of Episcopalians in America to be consecrated in England, and he was the first bishop of any denomination to exercise jurisdiction in the United States. Yet from a purely sacramental perspective, the statement needs some amendment. Seabury was the third clergyman consecrated for service in America.

John Talbot (1645-1727) was one of the two men consecrated before Seabury. Originally a ship's chaplain, Talbot had been persuaded to enter the service of the Society for the Propagation of the Gospel (SPG) by George Keith. Keith, a former Quaker who became the SPG's first missionary in 1702, was a passenger on the ship for which Talbot served as chaplain. By the time that ship had completed the trip from England to America, Talbot was interested enough in the work of the SPG to resign his chaplaincy and to volunteer for service with the society. He joined Keith in a two-year missionary tour of the colonies and then settled down to serve a congregation in Burlington, New Jersey.

Like many other early missionaries for the SPG, Talbot became convinced that the Anglican Church in the American colonies needed a resident bishop. SPG officials back in England agreed. They lobbied the parliament and Queen Anne for a colonial bishop. At the time of Anne's death in 1714 they were near success, for Anne had asked the parliament for colonial bishops. Anne's successor, George I, showed no interest in the colonial episcopate, however, and the new parliament he summoned in 1718 was openly hostile. Society members eventually abandoned the project.

Talbot, however, refused to give up on the idea. When he visited England in 1720 in order to apply for retirement funds, he discussed the problem with others. Apparently, about this time he made contact with a nonjuring priest by the name of Robert Welton. Welton, like other members of the first generation of nonjurors, was an Anglican clergyman who refused to acknowledge the accession of William and Mary to the English throne in the Glorious Revolution of 1688. As a result of his refusal, the government had removed him as the rector of Whitechapel in London.

The lot of the nonjurors was far more difficult in the 1720s than it would be at the time of Seabury's consecration two generations later. With James Stuart's son ("Old Pretender" James III, 1688-1766) and grandson ("Bonnie Prince Charles," 1720-88) still entertaining hopes of regaining the English crown, the British authorities equated the nonjurors' dogged refusal to pray for the sitting monarch as an act of political rebellion. The nonjurors, therefore, had to be extremely cautious about their activities. Even so, they often found themselves in English prison.

Despite the possible political risks involved, however, Welton suggested to Talbot that nonjuring bishops might be persuaded to consecrate both himself and Talbot as bishops for the American colonies. The bishops that Welton initially approached responded in the negative. Talbot, they pointed out, was not a nonjuror and Welton's moral life had been less than exemplary.

Welton persisted, however. Finally, in the summer of 1722 he convinced nonjuring Bishop Ralph Taylor to consecrate. Taylor, who had himself been consecrated in the preceding year, was in poor physical and mental health. He would die before the year was out. Against the advice of his fellow nonjuring bishops, he went ahead with the service. Bishop Taylor apparently held the service in secret and, contrary to the tradition that three bishops preside at a consecration, acted alone.

When John Talbot returned to the colonies later that year, he was unsure how to proceed. Nonjurors, he soon discovered, were no more welcome in the British colonies than they were in England. When Talbot revealed his consecration to a group of Connecticut candidates for ordination to the diaconate who were preparing to sail to England, they rejected his offer to ordain them. After this and perhaps other rebuffs, Talbot decided to remain quiet about his consecration. He seemed not to have told the parishioners of the congregation to which he returned in New Jersey.

Robert Welton, however, chose another course of action. Arriving in Philadelphia in 1724, he convinced the vestry of Christ Church to employ him as interim rector. He told others of the consecration, demanded their obedience, and began even to question the legitimacy of the ordination of clergy who had not been ordained in the nonjuring line.

A disgruntled clergyman by the name of John Urmstone, who had been previously discharged by the Christ Church vestry, wrote to the SPG. The missionary society responded immediately in the case of Talbot, who at that point was the missionary with the longest record of service with the society. Before 1724 was over the society cut off his salary and pension and wrote to his colonial governor, who ordered him to halt the exercise of his ministry. Talbot appealed to the society, citing his years of service and saying that he had never entertained nonjuring sentiment. He died in 1727, unable to convince the SPG to change its decision.

Since he was not under the authority of the SPG, Welton was able to survive slightly longer. The government acted more slowly than the SPG. It was not until January of 1726 that he received an order demanding that he return to England. Fearing the possibility of imprisonment, he fled in another direction. He went to Lisbon, Portugal, and apparently died soon afterwards.

When Bishop Samuel Seabury was in Scotland for his nonjuring consecration almost sixty years later, he apparently learned of the consecration of Talbot and Welton. Not surprisingly, however, he did little to call attention to the similarities of their consecration and his own.

Edward LeGare Pennington carefully sifted the limited evidence about the two early bishops in his Apostle of New Jersey: John Talbot *(Philadelphia: Church Historical Society, 1938).*

Unsuccessful Social Satire

In the 1760s, New England Congregational clergy mounted an attack in the press and from the pulpit on what they regarded as a new threat to their denominational hegemony—the Anglican Church. In the seventeenth century, New England had been settled by Puritans, members of reforming party intent on "purifying" the practice of the Church of England. But events in England in the middle of that century—the Puritan Commonwealth and the Restoration of Charles II—had redrawn denominational lines. The Puritans had become the modern Congregationalists, and the Anglicans were represented in New England only by a few scattered congregations of sailors and other later immigrants.

Missionaries sent to minister to those congregations made modest gains in the first half of the eighteenth century, with their most notable success the 1722 conversion of the faculty of Congregational Yale College. Even with these gains, Congregationalists considered Anglicans more of an annoyance than a major threat to the standing order.

The situation began to change, however, in the 1740s. Anglican George Whitefield, Congregationalist Jonathan Edwards, and Dutch Reformed pastor Theodore Frelinghuysen preached a series of revival sermons that led to a Great Awakening among American Christians. Itinerant preachers carried the message of revival to every colonial town, and individuals began to profess their conversions in increasing numbers.

Paradoxically, the Anglican congregations in New England began to attract both those who favored the awakening and those who had reservations about it. On one hand, such Anglican clergy as Samuel Peters of Hebron, Connecticut, supported Whitefield and the Awakening. On the other hand, Anglican churches offered a fixed liturgy that guaranteed order even in the excitement of revival.

By the 1760s, New England Congregational clergy became alarmed by the steady loss of parishioners. Boston clergyman Jonathan

Mayhew launched the initial salvo against the Anglican Church. Joined by Charles Chauncy, Noah Welles, and others, he began to satirize the Anglican Church as an exclusive social club, more concerned with appearances than piety. In one pamphlet, Mayhew included a picture of the home of well-to-do Anglican clergyman East Apthorp. An inscription below the picture queried whether this was to be a bishop's palace. In another pamphlet, Welles pretended to be a pompous Anglican clergyman.

Together they painted a picture of the Anglican Church as a church for the rich. The charge was true only in a very limited sense. Some wealthy members of the Congregational church had joined the Anglican Church during the Great Awakening. By and large, however, the Anglican clergy in New England ministered to parishioners who were markedly less well off than the established Congregationalists. Anglicans in New England were, for example, more likely to live in rural areas and were more often found on the tax lists as indigent.

Whatever the fairness of the charge, however, it seemed unable to stem the growth of the Anglican Church in New England. The denomination continued to increase in numbers, even despite the considerable disadvantage of association with England in the Revolution. Anti-Anglican sentiment quieted within the Congregational Church following the Revolution, and for most of the following century relations remained cordial between the two denominations. Ironically, one of the leaders of the Episcopal Church in that century would be Jonathan Mayhew's namesake and grandson, Bishop Jonathan Mayhew Wainwright of New York.

A New Name

Anglicans in the American colonies during the Revolutionary War found themselves in an uncomfortable position. The very title of their denomination—the Church of England—included the name of the nation with whom they were at war. For some Anglicans—loyalists who sided with the British—this was not a problem, but for numerous patriots it was a constant source of embarrassment.

The church in Maryland was the first to attempt a solution to this quandary. In 1783 the clergy in the state, meeting in Annapolis, adopted a new name—the Protestant Episcopal Church.

Though the Maryland clergy were the first to use the word *Episcopal* as part of the title of their church, the term already had a long history. Derived from the Greek word for bishop (*episkopos*), the word had been used by English speakers since the fifteenth century to mean "of or pertaining to a bishop." In the seventeenth century, English Christians had begun to refer to an "Episcopal party" within their national church. Members of that party, in contrast to Presbyterians and Congregationalists, favored a church polity with the three traditional orders of ordained clergy (bishops, priests, and deacons).

Presbyterians favored abolition of the bishops and the formation of presbyteries, bodies in which priests (presbyters or elders) met as equals. Presbyterians gained the upper hand during the English Civil War (1642-52), but the Episcopal party eventually triumphed with the restoration of Charles II in 1660, ensuring an episcopal government for the Church of England.

In the period before the American Revolution there were no Anglican bishops in the colonies. The American press, however, used the noun *Episcopalian*, to refer to Anglican advocates of an American episcopate, such as Thomas B. Chandler (1726-90). When Anglican clergy met after the Revolution, the question of the episcopate was foremost in their minds. The term *Episcopal* was a logical expression of their hopes of success in obtaining bishops; theirs was to be the church with bishops.

The Maryland clergy had also included the word *Protestant* in their title, a testimony to the fact that they were meeting in the state with the largest Roman Catholic population. Roman Catholics were also interested in obtaining an episcopate; five years after the consecration of an American Episcopal bishop, John Carroll would become the first Roman Catholic bishop of Baltimore. The word *Protestant* would allow no confusion between the efforts of the two denominations. Anglicans wanted a Protestant episcopate.

The title was quickly accepted by Americans in other states. The Anglican clergy and laypersons who met in the first General Convention in Philadelphia in 1785 adopted the Maryland name with the addition of the phrase "in the United States of America." The name of the new republic had displaced that of the old colonial power.

The Protestant Episcopal Church in the United States of America was the first independent Anglican Church outside of the British Isles. As other Anglican provinces gained their independence, some have followed the American pattern in their choice of a title (the Episcopal Church of Brazil, the Episcopal Church in Jerusalem and the Middle East). Others have retained the word *Anglican* (the Anglican Church of Canada, the Anglican Church of the Southern Cone of the Americas), while still others have taken the name of the nation in which they are located (the Church in the Province of Burma, the Church in the Province of Nigeria, the Church in the Province of Papua New Guinea).

American Methodists have also made use of the word *Episcopal*. The Methodists, who began as a movement within the Anglican Church, met in Maryland the year following the Maryland clericus in order to draw up an organization plan. They adopted the name the Methodist Episcopal Church. Though the United Methodists dropped the word *Episcopal* in a 1939 merger of branches that had divided over the Civil War, four nineteenth-century offshoots of Methodism still retain the word *Episcopal* in their names: the African Methodist Episcopal Church, the African Methodist Episcopal Zion Church, the Christian Methodist Episcopal Church, and the Reformed Methodist Union Episcopal Church.

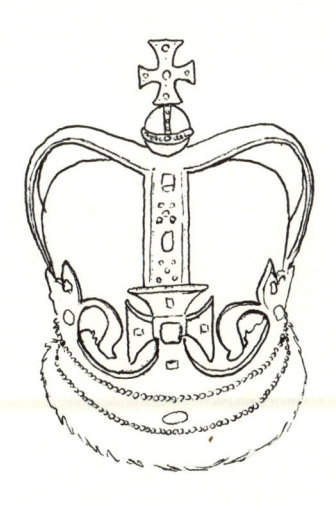

The Ordination of Weems and Gantt

Many Episcopalians know the story of the ordination to the episcopate of Samuel Seabury, the first American bishop. Few, however, are acquainted with the story of the first two Americans to be ordained to the priesthood after the Revolution. Like Seabury, they traveled to England. Unlike him, they were successful in England and did not have to move on to Scotland for ordination.

Both young men were from Maryland. The Anglican Church in Maryland, as in Virginia, the Carolinas, Georgia, and four counties of New York, was the established church during the years leading up to the American Revolution. The state legislature created new parishes, the governor chose the parish rectors, and the landowners supported the church with annual tithes. This harmonious relationship ended with the Revolution, however. American patriots were extremely uncomfortable with a church whose liturgy included prayers for George III. The Maryland legislature suspended the tithes paid to the Anglican Church and began to arrest clergy who insisted on praying for the king.

When the fighting ended in America, Anglicans in Maryland attempted to reorganize their denomination. No longer the established church, they needed to choose a form of government that would allow them to function independently of the governor and the legislature. With no formal ties to England, they needed to plan for a resident bishop.

Dr. William Smith, a former provost of what is today the University of Pennsylvania who had moved to northern Maryland during the British occupation of Philadelphia, led the way in this organizational effort. Smith became a proprietor of the Kent School in Chestertown and within a few years transformed it from a boys' school to a college named after George Washington. He used an early graduation ceremony to contact Anglican clergy and laity. Beginning in 1780, he chaired statewide meetings that obtained a state charter for the church, secured ownership of some church property, and elected a candidate for bishop.

Those who attended the early state conventions with Smith knew that the state was badly in need of clergy. Before the war there were more than forty-five Anglican clergy in Maryland. By 1782 only nine were left. The delegates to the convention felt that ordination of new clergy was a central priority for the reorganized church. Delegates sensed that consecration of bishops for the American church was still a long way off. To be ordained, candidates would still have to travel to England. Delegates designated a committee to examine potential ordinands. The committee's first choices were Mason Locke Weems and Edward Gantt, Jr. Both were twenty-three and had been Anglicans since infancy. Weems, who was a cousin of Mrs. William Smith, was from Anne Arundel County. He had graduated from the Kent School and had studied at a Scottish university. Gantt was from Calvert County.

The two sailed for England even before that nation had agreed to peace terms. When the English would not allow the American ship in which they sailed to land, they were forced to travel to France. They waited there until English and American representatives in Paris negotiated a peace treaty.

By the end of 1782 they had reached England. Yet their troubles had just begun. When they presented themselves to the English bishops for ordination, they learned that the English parliament had not dispensed with the requirement that all ordinands swear allegiance to George III. Gantt and Weems knew that their priesthood would mean little at home if it had been secured with an oath to the British monarch. They had little choice other than to await some further action by parliament.

Within a year, they were joined by Samuel Seabury. Seabury was a New York priest who had been elected as a candidate for bishop by the clergy of Connecticut. The Connecticut clergy had heard of the efforts of Maryland Anglicans and probably knew of Weems and Gantt's trip. Maryland Anglicans believed that Americans needed to organize a national church structure before petitioning the English for consecration of bishops; they sent candidates for the priesthood to England but would await the organization of General Convention before considering sending a candidate for the episcopate. The Connecticut clergy disagreed; they believed that only bishops could lead the way in the formation of a national church. Not waiting for assurances that consecration was a real possibility, Seabury had sailed for England. He arrived in England in 1783. Once there he learned that the oath of allegiance was still required. Like Weems and Gantt before him, he had to await the action of the parliament.

On August 13, 1784, the parliament acted. Their Enabling Act allowed for the ordination of American deacons and priests without an oath of allegiance. Taking advantage of the new legislation, the bishop of Chester ordained Mason Locke Weems and Edward Gantt, Jr. to be the diaconate on September 5. One week later, the archbishop of Canterbury ordained them to the priesthood. Soon after, they returned to the church in Maryland, which so badly needed their help.

Seabury, however, was less pleased with the result of parliament's labors. That legislative body provided for the ordination of deacons and priests, but it did not provide for the consecration of bishops. The parliament was still unsure about the reception that an Anglican bishop would receive in the United States. Presbyterians, Congregationalists, and even some Anglicans had vigorously opposed plans to send a bishop in the prewar years, seeing in such proposals another attempt at British domination. Moreover, they had some doubts about the manner of Seabury's election. He was chosen in a secret meeting of clergy that included no laypersons. How would the laity of Connecticut react to the consecration of a bishop?

Samuel Seabury abandoned all hope of favorable parliamentary action and went to Scotland, where a nonjuring Scottish church functioned independently of parliament. The nonjurors hadn't accepted the deposition of James II a century before and believed all subsequent English governments to be illegitimate. Three nonjuring bishops consecrated Samuel Seabury on November 14, 1784.

Gantt and Weems were successful in their efforts to secure ordination. They would, however, be the last Americans to visit England for ordination to the priesthood. For after Seabury's return to Connecticut in 1785, it became possible for ordination to take place in the United States. Others would, however, travel to England for consecration to the episcopate. In June of 1786 the British parliament dropped its objection to consecration of American bishops. Two Americans were consecrated in England in 1787, and a third was consecrated three years later, giving the Americans the traditional three bishops required for the continuation of apostolic succession.

Thus, four Americans had visited England in search of consecration to the episcopate. One had failed, and three had been successful. It was, however, Gantt and Weems who had come first. Undoubtedly, their success had contributed in some small way to the consecrations that followed.

The Free African Society

The black members of St. George's Methodist Episcopal Church were angry. Freed blacks in Philadelphia had joined the congregation precisely because of the real possibility of black leadership. Now, however, white members had publicly insulted the black Sunday school teachers Absalom Jones (1746-1818) and Richard Allen (1760-1830), the informal spokesmen for the black membership of the parish. Blacks, aware of the promises of liberty in the recently adopted Declaration of Independence, were unwilling to accept such treatment.

On the surface, the argument was about seating in the church. White members, meeting separately, had decided that blacks should sit only in the balcony. They had not, however, informed black parishioners of their decision. Black members of the congregation arrived for worship on a Sunday in 1786 and sat in their accustomed places in the nave. White ushers singled out Jones and Allen and during their opening prayers asked them to move to the balcony. The triple insult—the white decision, and lack of advanced notification, and the request to move that interrupted their devotions—was more than Jones and Allen could bear. They vacated their seats as requested, but rather than moving to the balcony, they walked out of the church. The other black members followed.

The blacks lacked a meeting place and were unsure what course of action to follow. They were certain of one thing, however—they would not again accept second-class treatment of the sort that they had just received. They formed an organization, which they named the Free African Society, to seek ways to promote the welfare of the growing black community in Philadelphia. They also were active in civic efforts that benefited all the citizens of the city. Jones, Allen, and the members of the Free African Society took a leading role, for example, in the caring for the sick when an epidemic struck the city.

Despite their success in such efforts, members of the Free African Society did not forget their initial focus on worship. After 1792, when they had begun to construct their own building, they began to seek affiliation with some existing American denomination. Members of the congregation looked in two possible directions: toward the Methodist Episcopal Church, which they had left, and toward the Episcopal Church. As the name Methodist Episcopal might indicate, the lines of division between the two denominations were not as clear as they later came to be. In the period between 1750 and 1785, Methodist societies functioned as prayer and study groups within the colonial Anglican Church. In 1785, however, Methodists, unwilling to wait for the relatively slow reconstitution of an American Episcopal Church, formed a separate denomination. For the remainder of the 1780s it was still common for Americans to switch back and forth between the two denominations.

Absalom Jones conferred with William White, the Episcopal bishop of Pennsylvania. White offered to accept the society as an independent Episcopal congregation. He promised the blacks would not be compelled to accept a white rector. Jones would serve as a lay reader, and, after a period of study and ordination, as rector of the parish. The majority of the parish agreed to the offer, and in 1794 the Free African Society of Philadelphia became St. Thomas Episcopal Church.

Not all members of the society accepted the decision, however. Richard Allen was convinced that the members should seek admission to the Methodist Episcopal Church as a congregation separate from St. George's Methodist Episcopal Church. In 1793 he left the Free African Society to form Bethel Church for Negro Methodists. In 1816 he left the Methodist Church to form a new denomination, the African Methodist Episcopal (AME) Church. Allen, ordained deacon by the Methodists in 1799 and elder in 1816, was the second American black ordained in a hierarchical denomination. Jones, whom Bishop White ordained deacon in 1795 and priest in 1804, was the first.

Absalom Jones and the hundreds of black Episcopal clergy who have followed after him have continued the tradition of social activism that began in the 1787 walkout at St. George's Church. At the time of his death, Jones was involved in organizing free blacks to oppose the effort of the white-run American Colonization Society to send freed slaves to Africa. Peter Williams, Jr., the first black Episcopal clergyman in New York, was so active in the abolition movement in the 1820s that whites burned down his church. At the century's end, Alexander Crummell organized the forerunner of the NAACP (the National Association for the Advancement of Colored People). The circumstances have changed over the decades, but the fierce conviction that moved the members of the Free African Society has not.

Weems, the Moral Reformer

In the early 1790s, a Maryland clergyman decided to transfer his endeavors from the pulpit to the printed page. Newly married and concerned about income, he certainly had doubts about the step that he was taking. Would he reach as many people with his writing as with his sermons? Was there a market for nonfiction in the new American republic? Yet his fears proved unfounded. To this day, the stories that he recounted are among the most well known in America.

The priest's name was Mason Locke Weems. After ordination to the priesthood in England in 1784, he had served in All Hallows and Westminster parishes in Maryland. It was after his marriage to Fanny Ewell of Prince William County, Virginia, in the early 1790s that he began to think about a career in writing.

Weems believed that he could make an important contribution to American life. At the end of the eighteenth century, American society was wide open with no holds barred. Alcoholic consumption, not only by adults, but also by children as young as eight or nine, was three times what it is today. Dueling was so popular that major cities all had their dueling grounds. Those who dueled included the leading citizens of the new nation. One Maryland clergyman with whom Weems was acquainted had even chased a pair intent on dueling into the White House. Both Vice President Aaron Burr and President Andrew Jackson would kill men in duels.

The loyalists who had left America during the American Revolution were among the most conservative citizens. With the loss of their calming influence and the departure of a British colonial government that saw itself at least in theory as responsible for the religious character of the nation, America existed in a kind of moral vacuum.

It was to this situation that Weems responded. Learning of a publisher through his cousins in Philadelphia, he proposed a book of sermons by Episcopal clergy. Then he hit upon a two-pronged scheme that would prove far more popular. On the one hand, he wrote pamphlets condemning the great sins of his day, which were illustrated with enough negative examples to make them interesting to his readers. They had such titles as *God's Revenge against Gambling*, *God's Revenge against Adultery*, *God's Revenge against Dueling*, *The Drunkard's Looking Glass*, and *The Bad Wife's Looking Glass*. On the other hand, he produced a series of biographies extolling the positive virtues of American leaders. He included volumes on George Washington, Francis Marion, William Penn, and Benjamin Franklin.

He divided his time between living at Bel Air, the Ewell family home in Virginia, and traveling the road, selling his books and those of others. An effective salesman as well as a writer, he earned a permanent place in American hearts for his works. Few in America today are unacquainted, for example, with the story of George Washington and the cherry tree, which Weems told in his biography of the first president. His message was a simple one—that personal morality is a necessity for a healthy nation—but it was one that Americans of the late eighteenth century needed to hear.

A Changing Episcopate

When Samuel Seabury of Connecticut, William White of Pennsylvania, Samuel Provoost of New York, and James Madison of Virginia were consecrated to the episcopate in Great Britain in the years from 1784 to 1790, the Anglican Church in North America was already almost two hundred years old. American Anglicans may have been committed to the principle of episcopal ministry, but before 1784 they had no practical experience with the institution. Quite naturally, therefore, they had a number of important questions to ask. How, for example, did the ministry of the bishop differ from that of the priest?

The generation of Anglicans that laid the foundations for the American Episcopal Church in the 1780s gave a cautious answer to the question. Many of them saw the ministry of the bishop as differing from that of the priest in only three regards: The bishop presided at diocesan conventions, confirmed, and ordained. Since most of the early bishops had served as presidents of diocesan conventions prior to their election, and few of them would visit parishes for confirmation, the only practical change that consecration brought was the power of ordination.

Virginia Episcopalians were perhaps the most explicit about this understanding. In 1785 the state's diocesan convention adopted a canon limiting the power of any future bishop to confirmation, ordination, and presidency of the convention. Both their reluctance to give authority to the bishop and their preoccupation with ordination were understandable. Americans had just fought a revolution against what they believed to be the excessive authority of the English monarch; they were not anxious to surrender their newly won independence to anyone.

The concern with ordination was also related to the recent war. Only a bishop could ordain. Since America had no resident bishops before 1784, candidates were forced to sail for England for ordination. After 1776, however, all such ordinations had ended. Travel to England was impossible. Moreover, even if candidates had arrived, English law would have required their oath of allegiance to King George III.

Nor was the cessation of ordinations the only cause of a clergy shortage. At the time of the Revolution, some clergy were recent arrivals from England. All had taken an oath of allegiance to the English monarch at the time of ordination, and all were required by canon law to read the daily Morning and Evening Prayer services, which contained a petition that King George "vanquish and overcome all his enemies." Roughly half of colonial clergy believed that they were conscience-bound to oppose the Revolution. They were harassed and, in some cases, imprisoned. When the war ended, many left for England, Canada, or Bermuda. The departure of clergy combined with the halt in ordinations to make the clergy shortage acute. Maryland, to use one example, had forty-five clergy before the Revolution; by 1782 there were only nine priests left in the state.

The first American bishops understood the critical importance of ordinations and did their best to meet the problem. Between 1791 and 1796, for example, Madison of Virginia ordained seventeen persons, Seabury of Connecticut ordained ten candidates, and Provoost of New York ordained a dozen. The initial bishops also served as parish rectors and had limited time to devote to the business of their dioceses. For most of them this preparation and selection of candidates for ordination and the regular meeting of diocesan and General Conventions consumed all of their available time. With the exception of Seabury, who died in 1796, they rarely visited parishes in their dioceses, generally did not confirm, and confined their pastoral ministry to their own congregations.

This early model of the episcopate met the immediate needs of the church. Yet by 1800, it was evident to some that an episcopate limited to ordination had real disadvantages. Once the clergy shortage had been remedied, the bishops had little else to offer to their dioceses. Some Episcopalians began to lose interest in the episcopate. In 1800, seven states had bishops, but by 1804 the number would drop to five. Moreover, no new bishops would be consecrated between that year and 1811. It would be the longest such gap in the history of the American church.

When the War of 1812 jarred Episcopalians—they were forced again to choose between patriotism and English roots—they would turn to a broader understanding of the role of the episcopate. Bishop John Henry Hobart of New York led the way in developing this broader view. Consecrated in 1812 as an assistant to the infirm

Bishop Benjamin Moore, he was not content simply to ordain and preside at diocesan convention. He began a process of regular parish visitation, addressed pastoral letters to the people of his diocese, raised funds for western missions, encouraged the formation of a seminary, played a role in placement of clergy, and wrote vigorously in defense of the church.

Other dioceses soon imitated Hobart's example. Virginia, for example, elected a New Yorker acquainted with Hobart's style of ministry as its second bishop. Still other dioceses chose candidates with even closer connections with Hobart; his son-in-law and six of his assistants at Trinity Church, New York City, would eventually be consecrated as bishops.

Bishops who understood their responsibility primarily in terms of the ability to ordain would soon become a thing of the past. Yet they had played a vital role in the history of the church. They had traveled to Great Britain to insure that the apostolic succession would be preserved in the Episcopal Church. All later American bishops can trace their lines of consecration through them. They had met the acute shortage of clergy. Moreover, they may well have provided the only model of leadership that patriotic Americans would have accepted in the years following the Revolution. Their modest beginnings laid the groundwork for the more vigorous episcopal style introduced by John Henry Hobart.

Robert Bruce Mullin's Episcopal Vision *(New Haven, CT: Yale Press, 1986) is an examination of Bishop Hobart's theology, which includes a thorough description of the bishop's episcopate.*

Episcopal Colleges

In 1775, American Anglicans could look with pride at their accomplishments in higher education. William and Mary College, founded in 1693 by James Blair, the bishop of London's official representative in Virginia, was the second oldest college in the thirteen colonies. Two newer institutions, the College of Philadelphia (1740) and King's College in New York (1754), were located in colonies in which the Anglican Church was either not established (Pennsylvania) or in which Anglican establishment was partial (New York with a four county "Protestant" establishment). The legislatures in those colonies were less willing to charter the schools as officially Anglican. Yet the administration, faculties, student bodies, and financial supporters of the institutions were predominantly Anglican. Trinity Church in New York City, for example, was the major financial backer of King's College.

The optimistic picture, however, changed rapidly with the onset of the Revolution. Some American patriots, unhappy with any remaining signs of British domination, regarded the efforts of the Church of England in higher education unfavorably. The General Assembly in Virginia abolished the professorship in divinity at the College of William and Mary. Patriots in New York changed the name of King's College to Columbia. Patriots in Pennsylvania countered the attempt of Anglicans to establish some official recognition of the Anglican character of the College of Philadelphia. Though many of the faculty continued to be Anglican clergy, the school, which was later renamed the University of Pennsylvania, became less and less Anglican in character. By the war's end, Episcopalians had no institutions of higher learning that they could call their own.

Disheartened by disestablishment, loss of English support for missionaries, and the popular opposition to the Church of England of many patriots, Episcopalians in most states were unable to reverse their losses in higher education in the years before 1820. Doubting that they would ever be able to regain schools with a denominational character, they supported existing state and private colleges. Bishops often served in the administration of such institutions. Bishops James Madison of Virginia, Robert Smith of South Carolina, Benjamin Moore of New York, and James Kemp of Maryland served respectively as the presidents or provosts of William and Mary (1775-1812), South Carolina College (1786-98), Columbia College (1801-11), and the University of Maryland (1815-27).

The one exception to this general rule was the state of Maryland. During the 1780s, Episcopalians there were able to transform secondary schools in Annapolis and Chestertown into St. John's and Washington Colleges. It was not until the 1820s that Episcopalians in other states were able to follow the Maryland example. New Yorkers founded Geneva (now Hobart) College in 1822. Episcopalians in Connecticut founded Washington (Trinity) College in 1823, and those in Ohio began Kenyon College the following year. South Carolinians brought Charleston College under the control of the Episcopal Church in the 1830s. Episcopalians in Tennessee began planning the University of the South in 1832, though the school would not actually open its doors until the 1860s. Members of the Episcopal Church in North Carolina founded St. Mary's (Junior) College for Women in 1842. Episcopalians in New York began Bard College in 1860, and those in Pennsylvania chartered Lehigh in 1865.

In addition to these successful institutions, Episcopalians were involved in a number of other efforts, whose results proved less permanent. This was particularly true in what were the then western states. Jubilee College (Illinois), Shelby College (Kentucky), St. Paul's College (Missouri), Racine College (Wisconsin), St. Andrew's College (Mississippi), St. Paul's College (Texas), and St. Mark's College (Michigan) all lived relatively short lives. Griswold College (Iowa) was somewhat longer lived.

In the years following the Civil War, Episcopalians continued to show their interest in building colleges, but they devoted their efforts in a new direction. Satisfied with the ability of existing institutions to educate upper-income white Americans, they focused on groups for whom college education was less available. Three colleges opened their doors for black Americans: St. Augustine's in North Carolina (1867), St. Paul's in Virginia (1888), and Voorhees College in South Carolina (1897). Episcopal philanthropist Martha McChesney Berry founded Berry College (1902) in Georgia for young men and women from Appalachia. Other Episcopalians brought higher education to the foreign mission field, creating such institutions as Cuttington

College in Liberia (1889), Trinity College in the Philippines, and Rikkyo University in Japan. A century later Carlos Plazas led the way in creating the bilingual Spanish-English St. Augustine College (1980) in Chicago.

Today most of the schools founded by Episcopalians exist as private colleges without any explicit ties to the Episcopal Church. Ten schools do, however, continue to identify themselves with the denomination through the Association of Episcopal Colleges. These ten are two of the overseas institutions (Cuttington and Trinity), the three black Colleges (St. Augustine's, St. Paul's, and Voorhees), the new bilingual school (St. Augustine), Hobart, Kenyon, Bard, and the University of the South.

Allen Gardiner

The Anglican Province of the Southern Cone, one of the Anglican Communion's newest members, celebrated its fifth anniversary in 1988. In that same year it also celebrated the one hundred and fiftieth anniversary of an event that has done much to determine the contours and character of the Anglican Church in Chile, Argentina, Uruguay, and Paraguay.

The event may not have seemed auspicious at the time. It was the decision of a former English sea captain by the name of Allen Gardiner to devote his time to evangelizing the Indians of Argentina and Chile. At the time of the Spanish conquest, the indigenous population of the southern portion of Latin America was in some ways similar to that in North America. The Indians were more mobile and less numerous than in the populous Indian cultures of Central America and Mexico. As in North America, European armies, diseases, and settlers displaced the original occupants from the more desirable lands and consigned them to a marginal role in colonial society. The tribes that still maintained their identity in the nineteenth century were largely ignored by public and religious institutions in the nations within whose borders they lived. Gardiner believed that they were forgotten peoples to whom he could make an important contribution.

Gardiner initially decided to minister to the Araucanos, a tribe that inhabited an area near the border between Argentina and Chile. To reach them from Argentina, he had to cross the Andes Mountains. The trip was a difficult one, and the Indians were not entirely receptive to his overtures. Discouraged but not defeated, he returned to Argentina.

Still convinced that his plan was workable, Gardiner began to prepare for a second mission. Realizing how vulnerable a lone missionary in the field could be, he contacted friends in England in order to form a new missionary society to support Anglican efforts in South America. Chartered in 1844, it was initially named the

Patagonian Missionary Society. Assured of outside support, Gardiner began a mission to the Yaganes Indians, who lived in the extreme southern tip of South America. He and five companions lived alongside of the Indians and shared their rugged life. In 1851 the six died as many of them would die—of hunger.

The missionary society that Gardiner had founded carried on his work after his death. The society, which changed its name to the South American Missionary Society (SAMS) in 1868 to reflect an expanding field of activity, also sent missionaries to the Araucanos with whom Gardiner had been unsuccessful and to the Indians of the Chaco region on the border of Argentina and Paraguay. Anglicans in Ireland, Australia, New Zealand, the United States, and other parts of the Anglican Communion would later form their own branches of SAMS to complement the original British effort.

In the twentieth century, the South American Missionary Society expanded its work to include non-Indians. This was particularly true after the Anglican bishops who gathered for a decennial conference in England in 1958 recommended expanding the ministry of the Anglican Church in South America to include all of the unchurched. Nonetheless, the character of the Anglican Church of the Southern Cone still bears the marks of Gardiner's original dream. Ninety-five percent of Paraguay's Anglicans are Lenguas Indians. Indians from the Chaco region make up a majority of the members of the Diocese of Northern Argentina, while those from the Temuco area make up an important part of the membership of the Diocese of Chile.

Phyllis Thompson's biography of Allen Gardiner, titled An Unquenchable Flame, *was published in London by Hodder and Stoughton in 1983.*

Charlotte Temple

By the middle of the nineteenth century the cemetery at Trinity Episcopal Church in New York City had become a tourist attraction. Thousands of visitors to the city made a point of stopping at the site. There were, to be sure, the graves of a number of distinguished persons at the church. A stately monument denoting a "patriot, soldier, and statesman" marked the place where first Secretary of the Treasury Alexander Hamilton had been buried after his infamous duel with Vice President Aaron Burr. The grave of American inventor Robert Fulton was at Trinity. Bishop John Henry Hobart and a host of other clerics were also buried there. It was not to these graves, however, that most of the visitors came. They came instead to a headstone erected to a person who may well have existed only in the pages of American fiction. It was the grave of Charlotte Temple.

Susanna Haswell Rowson (c. 1762-1824) created Charlotte Temple back in 1791, when she wrote what was to become America's first best-selling novel. Originally titled *Charlotte: A Tale of Truth*, it was the story of Charlotte Temple, a young English girl who, misguided by the false advice of her French teacher and lured by a handsome face and a smart uniform, sailed for America with a young soldier who promised to marry her. When the ship reached New York, however, the soldier lost interest in his promises. He married another, leaving Charlotte pregnant and friendless. Her loving father sailed from England to help but was too late. Charlotte, weakened by poverty and remorse, died in childbirth. Only then did her false lover see the error of his ways. He ended his days in melancholy, spending much of his time at her graveside.

Many of the elements of the story were based on events in Mrs. Rowson's own life. Her mother had died soon after her own birth. Her father was a British Navy officer who brought his family members with him to America but returned to England in poverty after capture in the American Revolution. Her husband, with whom she came to America a second time in the 1790s, was an undependable sort who served for a time with the Royal English Horse Guards. Like Charlotte's lover in the novel, he fathered an illegitimate child. In the book, Charlotte was left with little financial and emotional support. The same seemed to have been true for Mrs. Rowson. Indeed, her writing was an important source of income for her extended family.

Mrs. Rowson did not, however, acknowledge her book as a work of fiction in which she had drawn on her own experiences. Instead, following a convention common among eighteenth-century authors, she explained to her readers that her tale was a true one for which she had changed only certain names and geographical locations.

The book was immensely popular both in England and the United States. It was published forty-five times before 1825 and continued to be widely read until the First World War. Readers, both female and male, were captivated by the tragic tale of the young girl who died as a result of one unwise decision. In time, some of the more avid readers began the search for the grave of the "real" Charlotte Temple.

Mrs. Rowson had set the conclusion of her story in New York City but did not identify the location of Charlotte's grave. Mrs. Rowson was herself active in the Episcopal Church, however. In the later portion of her life she lived in Boston, where she attended Trinity Church. Thoughtful readers put this information together and decided that Charlotte's burial must have been at Trinity Church in New York City.

Sometime during the middle of the century, a gravestone marked "Charlotte Temple" appeared in the Trinity graveyard. Contemporary historians have not been able to determine whether the name was a mere coincidence or whether the headstone was the work of a Rowson fan. Charlotte Temple readers were, however, unconcerned with such details. They began to visit the graveside in droves, leaving flowers and small tokens of their own lost loves.

Temple fans continued to visit the grave in large numbers until the beginning of the twentieth century. By that time a second grave in the churchyard had begun to attract sizeable numbers of visitors; each December, crowds began to visit the final resting place of Clement Clarke Moore. In 1911, the clergy of Trinity parish organized an annual Christmas Eve procession for the children of Trinity Church to the grave of the author of the familiar Christmas poem.

Oxford University Press republished an inexpensive paperback edition of Charlotte Temple *in 1986.*

Giving the Clerk the Ax

One of the most lasting liturgical reforms in the American church was brought about by a young priest wielding an ax. The priest was William Augustus Muhlenberg (1797-1877); the setting, the early nineteenth-century Episcopal Church in Pennsylvania.

Muhlenberg was a great-grandson of Lutheran patriarch Henry M. Muhlenberg (1711-87). His family had entered the Episcopal Church as a result of a dispute among Philadelphia Lutherans over the use of English. German immigrants had brought worship in their native language with them to the American colonies. By the late eighteenth century, however, many second- and third-generation Lutherans were better versed in English than German. Lutheran congregations divided over the language question, one faction favoring retention of German, another advocating adoption of English. William Muhlenberg's parents objected to the resultant rancor and joined the United Episcopal Parish of Philadelphia.

William White (1748-1836) was rector of the parish. He was also the bishop of the diocese and the presiding bishop of the Episcopal Church. He took a liking to the Muhlenberg family and watched as William grew up in the church and attended the school at which one of his assistants taught. After graduation from college, Muhlenberg presented himself to Bishop White as a candidate for ordination. White prescribed a course of study and, upon its completion, ordained Muhlenberg.

In his first parish, Muhlenberg clashed with the clerk. The institution of parish clerk was a common one in the early nineteenth century. The clerk sat at a prayer desk in the front of the church building and led the congregation in its responses. Where prayer books were scarce or literacy low, the clerk was to help teach the congregation the service. Muhlenberg found, however, that the clerk in his parish had come to fill a very different role. He had become a replacement for congregational response. The worship service became a series of exchanges between two persons in the chancel.

Muhlenberg began to preach to his congregation about the importance of participation. Was not the liturgy the common possession of the People of God? Was not the clerk there to assist, rather than to replace, congregational response? The clerk, however, had different ideas. Perhaps fearing the loss of his salaried position, he resisted the priest's efforts. The more Muhlenberg urged the congregation to respond, the more the clerk increased his volume to drown out their voices.

In desperation, Muhlenberg sought the advice of Bishop White. Would he have the bishop's support if he were to remove the clerk's desk from the chancel? When White gave his consent, Muhlenberg set about his plan. Coming to the church building during the week, he tried to remove the desk. When it proved either too heavy or too firmly attached to the floor, Muhlenberg was undeterred. He took an ax and chopped the desk to pieces.

On Sunday morning the astonished clerk had no choice but to sit in the congregation. Robbed of his prominent location, he no longer presented an obstacle to congregational response. Muhlenberg's congregation began to participate more vigorously in the services. Their "clerkless" worship soon spread elsewhere in the church. Clerks and their desks began to disappear from chancels throughout the country, and soon they were only a distant memory.

For more information on Muhlenberg, see Alvin W. Skardon's Church Leader in the Cities *(Philadelphia: University of Pennsylvania Press, 1971).*

A Letter to the Presiding Bishop

She knew that to many it made no sense. She was married, and none of the married women in her neighborhood worked outside of the home. She was an Episcopalian, and the Episcopal Church's General Convention had not yet approved the ordination of women to the priesthood. Yet she was so sure. She was convinced that the Holy Spirit was calling her to the ordained ministry.

She shared her thoughts with her mother. She talked about her understanding of her call with her husband. They both were helpful, but neither could give her the answers that she wanted. Finally, she decided to take the matter up with a church official. She had heard that the presiding bishop was an advocate of minority rights; he had spoken up for Native Americans, for blacks, and for the deaf. Perhaps he would also be supportive of a woman who was certain of a call to the ordained ministry.

She wrote her first letter on August 18 and waited anxiously for a reply. It came within two weeks, but the answer was not the one for which she hoped. The presiding bishop was cordial enough, but he was not supportive of her hopes for ordination. The bishop pointed out that individuals were often mistaken about strong impressions of the leading of the Holy Spirit. He cautioned that her call might be delusory. He urged her to read the Bible.

She read and reread the presiding bishop's letter. She followed his advice and examined the Bible for evidence about the ministry of women. At first she was discouraged, but by the end of the week she was ready to write the bishop again. The presiding bishop and others had warned she would be abandoning her family responsibilities if she were ordained. Indeed, she admitted, she might inconvenience her family if she were to pursue her plans for ordination. But hadn't Jesus said in Matthew that the one "who loves son or daughter more than [him] is not worthy of [him]"? Moreover, why was there such a problem with women's ordination in the Episcopal

Church? Didn't Quaker women speak in church meetings? She mailed her letter on September 9.

This time she had to wait three weeks for the presiding bishop's reply. He conceded a number of points to her: Quaker women had preached; New Testament passages did not limit the gift of the Holy Spirit to males; Jesus did put faith before family in Matthew 10. On the central question, however, the bishop still held his ground. The gifts of the Holy Spirit and the forsaking of family in the New Testament were special circumstances that did not apply in modern times. The woman should look, not to the female prophets of the New Testament (Luke 2:36; Acts 21:9), but to Paul's specific injunction to the Corinthian women (1 Cor. 14:34) for her model. Women were to be silent in church.

The woman saw little point in continuing her correspondence with the presiding bishop. He had given some ground, but she knew that she could never convince him to ordain her. With no support from him or others, she stopped talking about her call. She found, however, that she could not stop thinking about it. Eight years later she was still convinced that ordination was the proper course for her to follow. She wrestled with periods of depression that resulted from her fear that she had disobeyed a direct calling from God.

There have been times in the life of the church in which a little waiting was all that was required to have closed doors open. Such was not the case for the troubled woman, however. She could not have lived long enough. For the year in which she first wrote to Presiding Bishop William White was 1811. Though the first Episcopal woman became a deaconness in 1845, the order was closed to married women until 1970. The General Convention opened the priesthood to women in 1976.

Bishop White must have been troubled by the correspondence with the woman. He saved copies of his letters to her for the rest of his life. His biographer, Bird Wilson, believed the exchange was significant enough to be included as an appendix in his 1839 biography of the bishop. Wilson chose, however, to keep the woman's identity anonymous.

Reversing an Episcopal Election

Episcopal elections are always important occasions in the life of the church. Clergy and laity gather in prayer to ask the guidance of the Holy Spirit in the selection of their leader. Multiple ballots are taken, and close votes are not unusual. But once the election is over, few question the outcome. With God's help, the people have a new bishop.

There are, however, exceptions to the usual scenario. One notable case was the Virginia election of 1812. Bishop James Madison had died in that year. Two months later, twelve laypersons and thirteen clergymen met in Richmond to elect his successor. There was broad agreement on one candidate, the Reverend John Bracken. Twenty-two of the twenty-five delegates present cast their votes for him.

To most, Bracken seemed a logical choice. Virginia's first bishop had served in the double role of bishop and president of the College of William and Mary. Before him, a series of colonial commissaries, representatives of the bishop of London, had combined supervisory responsibilities in the church with the presidency of William and Mary. Bracken, who had spent thirty-seven years as a professor at William and Mary, was respected at the college and had already been elected to fill the vacancy in the presidency created by Bishop Madison's death. At sixty-five years of age Bracken was a safe and logical choice. Yet Bracken would never be consecrated bishop. Stranger still, it would be a recently ordained deacon, a young man with little experience in the church, who would change the outcome of the election.

His name was William Meade. From Frederick County, Virginia, he was serving at the time as the rector of Christ Church, Alexandria. He understood the rationale for the diocesan vote but was convinced that Virginia did not need another college president as bishop. Bishop Madison had been a sincere and devout man, but it seemed to Meade that for him the episcopate had taken a back seat to his college responsibilities. Indeed, in the final years of his life, Madison had not even called the annual meetings of diocesan council.

Meade wanted a younger, more vigorous man, a candidate with extensive experience and success in parish ministry. He persuaded William Holland Wilmer, then newly arrived from Maryland as the rector of St. Paul's, Alexandria, and a few others of the wisdom of his argument. They had no canonical basis on which to invalidate the election of Bracken. They did, however, have considerable powers of persuasion. They formed a delegation to approach Bracken and suggest to him that he decline election as bishop. He agreed, and a second election was scheduled for 1814.

By the time of the election, Meade and Wilmer had a strong candidate of their own. Through a friend in Maryland they had heard of Richard Channing Moore, the fifty-one-year-old rector of St. Stephen's Church in New York. Moore had twenty-seven years of successful parish work behind him, and though his congregation was rapidly growing, Meade and Wilmer believed that he might be persuaded to leave his charge and come to Virginia.

In the early part of the nineteenth century, the episcopate was still a part-time job. Bracken was to have divided his time between college presidency and the episcopate. If Moore were to come to Virginia, he would also need a second position. The persuasive Meade and Wilmer convinced the congregation of Monumental Church in Richmond to call Moore as rector, if he were also elected bishop by diocesan convention. The church was Richmond's newest congregation, with a building constructed on the site of a terrible theatre fire that had killed seventy-two persons in 1811. Wilmer and Meade convinced diocesan convention to elect Moore, and the Monumental congregation responded as promised. In 1814, Moore accepted both calls and was consecrated as the second bishop of Virginia.

Meade and Wilmer's intervention in the election of 1812 changed the character of the church in Virginia. Moore soon presided over a major revival. He brought gifts different from those of a distinguished college professor, but they seemed to be precisely those gifts needed to bring life to the diocese. He had an engaging preaching style, an organizational ability, and a pastoral sensitivity that enabled him both to harness the enthusiasm of men like Meade and Wilmer and to draw an increasingly broad portion of the membership of the church into the work of renewal. He requested and received an assistant at Monumental Church so that he could spend more time visiting other parishes of the diocese. He participated in the founding of a theological seminary in Alexandria in order to provide needed candidates for the ministry, and he encouraged diocesan societies for missionary work and Christian education.

Meade and Wilmer would both go on to assume positions of importance. Paradoxically, Wilmer would be elected president of William and Mary. Meade would learn what it was to be the object of a closely contested episcopal election. In 1827, the Diocese of Pennsylvania came within one vote of choosing him as bishop. When multiple ballots proved unable to break the deadlock, the convention elected a compromise candidate. Meade was, however, elected to the episcopate in Virginia in the following year.

Frontier Bishops

In the early decades of the nineteenth century, American pioneers were moving off the eastern seaboard, out of the original thirteen states to the west of the Appalachian Mountains, where land was still inexpensive and wild game plentiful. This western movement presented Episcopalians with an interesting problem. When they had organized as an American denomination in the 1780s, they had been concerned with settled areas where the Anglican Church had been planted before the Revolution. The situation in the West, however, was quite different. There were no long-standing parishes whose clergy and laity could be relied upon to organize a diocesan structure. How was the church to be expanded in the West?

In the years from 1817 to 1835, three individuals provided one solution to this problem. The three were Philander Chase (1775-1852), Benjamin Bosworth Smith (1793-1884), and James Hervey Otey (1800-63). Chase, Smith, and Otey were priests who began their ministries on the east coast. Chase served in parishes in New York and Connecticut; Smith in Massachusetts, Virginia, Vermont, and Pennsylvania; Otey in North Carolina. All three, however, sensed the great potential of the American West and left their settled parishes.

Chase was the first of the three to move west. He settled in Ohio in 1817. Making contact with Episcopal laypersons and the few clergy who had preceded him, he organized a series of missions and summoned a diocesan convention. The delegates to the convention recognized his zeal and his ability in organizing the church. They elected him bishop, and in 1819 he was consecrated the first bishop of Ohio.

Smith crossed the mountains in 1832, settling in Lexington, Kentucky. Otey left the Carolinas for Tennessee about the same time. They were, like Chase, able to provide an enthusiasm and an organizational ability that were badly needed. Smith was elected bishop of Kentucky in 1832 and Otey, of Tennessee, in 1834.

Serving as a bishop to a frontier diocese was, however, a mixed blessing. Frontier bishops had little income, great needs, and a severe shortage of clergy. With little support from the East, Chase, Smith, and Otey were forced to rely on their own resources. All three approached the problem in the same way. They followed the example of some eastern bishops who combined teaching positions with the episcopate. There were, however, no existing institutions to employ them, so they founded educational institutions of their own. They hoped that the schools would meet two needs: the shortage of clergy and their lack of an income. New graduates of the schools could be ordained, and the bishops could draw partial salaries for their work.

Some of the institutions that the three founded still exist today. Chase's Kenyon College (Gambier, Ohio) and Bexley Hall Seminary (now in Rochester, Ohio), Smith's Episcopal Theological Seminary in Kentucky (Lexington; it closed in the nineteenth century but reopened in 1951), and University of the South (Sewanee), of which Otey was one of the original planners, all still prepare candidates for the ordained ministry.

Western bishops who followed these three pioneers would, however, exercise their episcopates in a slightly different pattern. In 1835 the General Convention approved the election of missionary bishops for the frontier. These bishops were paid by the national church's Domestic and Foreign Missionary Society. They were, therefore, able to spend less time in creating educational institutions and proportionately larger periods on the founding of new congregations. The pioneer trio had, however, made the work of the new missionary bishops possible both by providing frontier seminaries and by calling the attention of the whole church to the needs of the West.

Charles R. Henery has edited a volume on frontier missions titled Beyond the Horizon. *It is available from Forward Movement.*

Holding the Reins of Revivalism

In the year 1823 a clergyman from the Diocese of Virginia wrote to his bishop for advice. Members of the clergyman's parish had become interested in various forms of religious exercise for which he could find no specific authorization in the *Book of Common Prayer*. These activities apparently included the formation of neighborhood groups for prayer and Bible study. Should he, the priest wanted to know, halt such activities or encourage them?

The priest's question was an important one. For most of the nineteenth century a continuing round of revivals, known collectively as the Second Great Awakening, moved throughout America. These revivals were sustained by the preaching of itinerate revivalists, such as Presbyterian Charles G. Finney (1792-1875), and by the continued meeting of parish prayer and study groups. For many American Protestants, the measures used by the itinerant revivalists—the setting aside of "anxious benches" for those worried about salvation, the naming in public prayers of those most in need of conversion, and the designation of a time in worship for personal testimony—became standard elements in their regular worship. But, as the bishop's correspondent noted, the prayer book included no such elements and no offices for use by neighborhood study groups. Should he, therefore, resist the inroads of Protestant revivalism in his parish?

The bishop to whom the priest had written was Richard Channing Moore (1762-1841), the second bishop of Virginia and a man with strong opinions on the subject. He answered by making a distinction between two modes of worship: "The Church has ordained services to be used in public, but certainly the Church does not mean to prevent her members from praying without form in private." Neighborhood prayer and study groups were private and could, the bishop suggested, adopt forms of worship not found in the prayer book. The priest could encourage such groups without compromising loyalty to the liturgy. Indeed, Moore argued, the effect of supporting the local prayer groups would be an increased attachment to the public forms of worship. "The people," Moore wrote, "seeing their minister disposed to afford them his countenance, instead of conceiving a dislike to our inimitable forms would become attached to them, and by an indulgence in private, would advocate them in public."

Before election as bishop, Moore had presided over prayer meetings in his own congregation. He was one of a number of figures who advocated formation of prayer and study groups in Episcopal parishes. Another important member of the group was Bishop Alexander Viets Griswold (1766-1843), whose parish study groups contributed to a well-known 1812 revival in Bristol, Rhode Island. The faculty of the Virginia Seminary also supported the idea, scheduling regular weeknight prayer meetings for students.

Bishop Moore included a piece of practical advice in his letter to the parish priest. "If I was so situated as to be convinced of its utility," he wrote of the prayer meetings, "I would keep the reins in my own hands. . . . When I say that . . . I mean that it should be done, if done at all, under my patronage."

Bishop Moore's letter is printed on pages 82-83 of J.P.K. Henshaw's Memoir of the Rt. Rev. Richard Channing Moore *(Philadelphia: William Stavely & Co., 1843).*

Kaiserswerth

In 1836 a Lutheran clergyman and his wife took a tentative step toward reviving a neglected church office. Before the century had passed, hundreds of others on four different continents imitated their effort. Their small beginning made a permanent impact on the Christian church.

Theodore (1800-60) and Frederica (1800-42) Fliedner were the couple. Theodore was the pastor of a Lutheran congregation in Kaiserswerth, a community near Dusseldorf, Germany. He and Frederica were overwhelmed by the seriousness of the social and economic problems facing the residents of Kaiserswerth. Many were recent arrivals from the countryside who came to the city in hopes of employment in the area's growing industry. They were unprepared for the hardships of city life. The situation was particularly difficult for women. Paid lower wages than male workers and stripped of the protection of family and friends, they often fell into crime and prostitution.

Theodore and Frederica did what they were able, but they found that their efforts alone were insufficient to meet the needs of their parishioners. Anxious to find a solution to the problem, Theodore traveled to England to visit homes for unmarried mothers and other institutions for women.

Theodore returned from the visit struck by the fact that women themselves did much of the work in those English institutions. He and Frederica began to see the work of those women as a ministry of the church that was as legitimate as anything that an ordained pastor undertook. Could this, they wondered, be properly the ministry of the deaconess?

St. Paul mentioned Phoebe, a deaconess in the church at Cenchreae, in his letter to the Romans (Rom. 16:1). For the following thousand years, deaconesses were active in the church. Around the eleventh century, however, the office of deaconess disappeared in the West, a victim of both a larger institution of female monasticism and of an increasingly hierarchical church structure. The institution survived for a longer period among the Eastern Orthodox Christians.

Deaconesses differed from nuns in several ways that were important to the Fliedners and other nineteenth-century Protestants. The office was biblical, while that of nun was not. Deaconesses, like Phoebe in Romans, identified with a congregation; they did not exercise their ministry through a separate monastic institution. The focus of a female diaconate was service, rather than the contemplation to which some orders of nuns devoted their attention.

The Fliedners knew that nineteenth-century German Lutherans would never consent to the reintroduction of female monasticism, which the Lutheran Church had eliminated at the Reformation. They suspected, however, the Lutherans might accept a revival of the female diaconate. Perhaps they could recruit a staff of female deacons to undertake social work in their parish.

In 1836 they convinced an unmarried woman in the parish named Gertrude Reichardt to enter the diaconate. Theodore Fliedner presided at a service or worship in which she was admitted to the order of ministry. Miss Reichardt moved in with the Fliedners and began active work with the poor and sick in the community. The word of her efforts spread rapidly. Other women entered the diaconate; soon they were too numerous to share the Fliedner's home. Christians elsewhere in Germany—including the Kaiser—began to contribute to the work of the deaconesses. Some wrote to the Fliedners asking them to assist in the formation of similar institutions elsewhere. By 1880 there were twenty-five places on four continents (Europe, Africa, Asia, and North America) where Lutheran deaconesses affiliated with Kaiserswerth were at work.

Not only Lutherans followed the Kaiserswerth example, however. Anglican, Baptist, and Methodist women also entered the female diaconate. Even the institution of female nursing owes much to the deaconesses at Kaiserswerth. Florence Nightingale (1820-1910), the pioneer of modern nursing, first learned about medical care from the deaconesses in that city.

Bishop Kemper's Plea

In 1840, Bishop Jackson Kemper (1789-1870) left his missionary jurisdiction for a brief visit to the east coast of the United States. Elected by the General Convention as the first missionary bishop just five years before, Kemper had already exercised his episcopate in a vast area that included Missouri and Indiana (his original charge); Illinois (where he filled in for an absent Bishop Philander Chase in 1837-38); Louisiana, Mississippi, Alabama, Georgia, and Florida (which he visited on a missionary journey originally planned by Bishop Otey of Tennessee); and Iowa and Wisconsin (added to his jurisdiction by the General Convention of 1838). In the later 1840s the energetic bishop would also devote his attention to Minnesota, Kansas, and Nebraska.

With such a large territory, Kemper faced a chronic clergy shortage. One of the purposes of his visit in 1840 was the recruiting of clergy for Wisconsin. He hoped to convince a few clergymen to return with him to serve in that portion of his jurisdiction. He recognized, however, that eastern recruits would never be able to fill all the vacancies on the frontier. He had, therefore, a second project in mind during his eastern tour. He hoped to raise contributions sufficient to underwrite the formation of a theological seminary in Wisconsin. Such an institution could prepare frontiersmen for the work of the church in the western states.

Kemper spoke at a number of well-established parishes. He had some success in raising funds for his proposed seminary, but he found no clergy willing to return with him. Settled clergy seemed little interested in leaving the relative comfort of the east coast for the wilds of Wisconsin. The missionary bishop did, however, have one other possible source of clergy. He went not only to ordained ministers, but also to the young seminarians at General Theological Seminary. Kemper requested and received permission to address the students there on the last Friday evening in May of 1840.

Kemper carefully prepared his remarks. He could have chosen to glamorize the work on the frontier or to emphasize the opportunities for advancement, but he did not. He chose instead to speak frankly of the difficulties involved. One of the second-year students, James Lloyd Breck, characterized the bishop's talk in a letter to his brother. Kemper warned, Breck wrote, "that the time was drawing nigh when persecution and suffering should again be the lot of Christ's ministers." The bishop sought only "self-denying men, men willing to . . . endure every species of hardship for the sake of Christ and His Church." Candidates for ordination unwilling to face such difficulties should not enter the ordained ministry at all. Those willing to undergo hardship in the West had an additional burden. Such men "must be willing to forego marriage for some years, and perhaps through life" (Charles Breck, *The Life of the Reverend James Lloyd Breck, D.D.* [New York: E. & J.B. Young & Co., 1886], pp. 7-8).

The bishop may have been discouraged with the initial response to his plea for clergy. Not a single member of the senior class agreed to serve in Wisconsin. The academic year was nearly over, and seniors had already made plans for ordination and parish work in the eastern dioceses in which they were also in short supply.

Kemper, however, succeeded in planting seeds in the hearts of some of the second-year students at General. Breck and six or eight members of the class began to talk among themselves about the possibility of moving to the West in order to create a new seminary there. Some of the students changed their minds or were unable to gain permission from their own bishops to undertake the work, but at the time of graduation the following year, Breck and two of his classmates—John Henry Hobart, Jr., and William Adams—were still committed to the western work. The three left for Wisconsin in August of 1841. Within a year they already had formed the beginning of what they would name Nashotah House Seminary.

Kemper's plea had not met with immediate success in 1840, but the seeds that he sowed had laid the groundwork for a new seminary and the possibility of a more adequate supply of clergy for the West.

Dr. Alexander Crummell

On an August night in the mid-1830s a group of fourteen black high school students huddled with their teacher in the dormitory of a small Canaan, New Hampshire, boarding school. Their school, newly founded by two abolitionists, was under siege. Local residents had branded the institution a public nuisance. They had already destroyed the school house, using yokes of oxen to drag it off its foundation and into a nearby swamp. Teacher and students awaited the return of the mob, gathering a few weapons and fearing the worst. At about 11:00 P.M. the mob returned. When one member of the mob fired on the building, Henry Highland Garnet, an older student who would later enter the ordained ministry of the Presbyterian Church, returned fire. The mob, unprepared for armed resistance, fled. The school would be closed—the students left the area within two weeks of the incident—but no lives were lost.

Another of the students would later enter the ordained ministry. His name was Alexander Crummell. Born in New York in 1819, he was the son of a free black woman and an African man who had been brought to America as a slave. He began his education at the parish school of St. Philip's Church, New York City, a black congregation founded in the year of his birth. After the aborted effort at secondary education in New Hampshire, he entered a school in Whitesboro, New York.

Crummell's teacher at the St. Philip's school was the Reverend Peter Williams, Jr., one of the sixteen black men ordained to the priesthood in the Episcopal Church before 1865. After completing his education at Whitesboro, Crummell decided to follow the path of his teacher. He applied for entrance in the General Theological Seminary and for candidacy for the ordained ministry in the Diocese of New York. Crummell was initially encouraged by General because of his strong academic qualifications. The administration of the school wavered, however, first discouraging him, fearing that his admission would jeopardize an expected $15,000 contribution from the Diocese of South Carolina, and then offering him admission on the condition that he would not live in, eat at, or sit inside the lecture halls of the seminary. He refused, and entered on a private course of studies for the ministry. He was ordained in 1844.

Crummell's ministry would be exercised on three continents. From 1848 to 1853 he was in England, first raising funds for African missions and then enrolled as a student at Cambridge University, from which he would receive a degree in 1853. While there he would be a popular speaker and preacher. From 1853 until 1873 he was a missionary in Liberia, where he served as the rector of a parish and as a college professor. In 1873 he returned to the United States to become rector of St. Luke's Church in Washington, D.C.

At St. Luke's, Crummell immediately became a leader in the Episcopal Church and in the black community. Among his multiple accomplishments were the publication of three books of sermons and lectures (*The Future of Africa*, *The Greatness of Christ*, and *Africa and America*, all of which are still in print) and the 1897 formation of the American Negro Academy (an educational endeavor that would be a forerunner of the NAACP). He also led the Conference of Church Workers among the Colored People, an Episcopal committee that successfully campaigned for higher educational standards for black clergy and against the adoption of regulations at the General Convention that would have, if adopted, removed blacks from participation in the leadership of the church.

Crummell was also a devoted parish priest. In his later years at St. Luke's, he became an informal placement agent who recommended black clergy to parishes.

Linkage, *a biannual publication covering current events and Afro-Anglican history, is available from the Office for Black Ministries, The Episcopal Church Center, 815 Second Ave., New York, NY 10017.*

The Renewal Theology of William Meade

In 1836, Bishop William White of Pennsylvania died. The only one of the first four bishops to be active in the national church after 1800, White had served as presiding bishop since 1795. Over his forty-one years in that office, he had written a church history, published volumes of lectures on the catechism and ordination, written on biblical subjects, and prepared a difficult theological tome. He was a visible sign of the unity of the church. While he lived, he was able to keep in balance the various strands and emphases within the church.

After Whites's death, however, Episcopalians broke into open debate about the nature of their church. How were they to relate to nonepiscopal Protestants? What did they believe about revivalism? What were they to think of the new ideas emanating from Oxford University in England? While members of the church offered a whole range of answers to these questions, they often fell into one of two broad camps: Evangelical Episcopalians stressed personal faith and commitment, while high-church Episcopalians stressed the catholic heritage of the church.

William Meade was the most vocal evangelical bishop engaged in this debate. First as the assistant bishop to an aging Richard Moore and then, after Moore's death in 1841, as the third bishop of Virginia, Meade championed the evangelical cause. He spoke at his diocesan convention and at General Convention. He stressed the importance of the church's evangelical heritage to the Virginia Seminary, of whose board of trustees he was chairman. He wrote and preached on the evangelical faith. When he felt that certain national organizations were in error, he participated in the formation of evangelical counterparts to those organizations; dissatisfied with the reading list of the Episcopal Sunday School Union, for example, he helped form the Protestant Episcopal Sunday School and Tract Society.

Two aspects of this church debate were deeply important to Meade. The first was ecumenism. Bishop Meade believed that Episcopalians should engage in cooperative efforts with other

Protestants. Most high-church Episcopalians disagreed. Other Protestants, they argued, did not approach God in the way that he had intended, that is, through episcopally ordained clergy. Their salvation was therefore in question. At best they could hope to reach God's kingdom through a back-door approach; they did not accept the proper terms of God's covenant but might receive his "uncovenanted" mercy. Meade strongly disagreed and did not hesitate to say so.

His second concern was with personal renewal. Meade was convinced that the renewal theology that had been important since the Great Awakening of the mid-eighteenth century should not be abandoned. According to this theological approach the Christian who had been baptized in infancy needed a conscious renewal of faith as an adult. When Christians made such a renewal, God would respond by renewing them in his image, thereby assisting them in living a Christian life. This renewal did not need to follow any single emotional pattern, but it was a necessary element of faith. There were no bishops in the United States at the time of the Great Awakening and, therefore, no office of confirmation. After their introduction, however, most Episcopalians saw confirmation as a particularly appropriate sign of adult renewal.

In the 1830s a group of theologians at Oxford University had begun to question the need for any such adult renewal. Edward Bouverie Pusey wrote in *Tracts for the Times*, for example, that a large portion of Anglican clergy erred in thinking that "justification is not the gift of God through his sacraments, but the result of a certain frame of mind, of a going forth of themselves and resting upon their Saviour." Such an understanding of renewal, Oxford theologians argued, would weaken the importance of the sacraments. Again, Meade would strongly disagree. A belief in renewal was vital to his understanding of the Christian faith.

In addition to these two issues of substance, the bishop also had strong opinions on the externals of worship. He favored un-ornate churches and simple liturgical practices. Stories—many apocryphal—still echo in the church about Meade's dislike for altars, his suspicion about crosses, and his rejection of the use of flowers.

Later generations have not followed Meade in matters of liturgy, but they have embraced the theological points that he made with such force. Meade would have been pleased to see the broad ecumenical participation of the Episcopal Church in this century. Moreover, he would detect signs of his own influence in the confirmation office in which the bishop now asks, "Do you renew your commitment to Jesus Christ?"

Thomas Gallaudet

To those with an interest in the education of the hearing-impaired, the name Gallaudet is a familiar one. Sophia Fowler Gallaudet was deaf. Her husband Thomas Hopkins Gallaudet opened the first permanent American school for the deaf (Hartford, Connecticut, 1817). Their son Edward founded the world's first college for the deaf (Gallaudet College, Washington, D.C., 1864), and their son Thomas taught at an institution for the deaf in New York City for fifteen years. Education was not, however, the only area in which members of the Gallaudet family would leave a lasting mark. They also led the way in the church's response to the deaf. This was particularly true of the younger Thomas Gallaudet.

During his years as a student at what is now Trinity College in Hartford, Connecticut, the younger Thomas Gallaudet began to express an interest in the Christian ministry. In many ways, that interest was not surprising; his father was a Congregational clergyman. Yet there was a difference; the college was an Episcopal institution, and, when Thomas began to think about ordination, he thought in terms of the Episcopal, rather than Congregational Church. He told his parents of plans to attend the Episcopal Seminary (General Theological Seminary) in New York City. He did not act upon those plans after his graduation from college in 1842, however. Acceding to the advice of his father, he began a career in teaching instead. He taught for a year in Connecticut and then in 1843 accepted a position at the New York (City) Institution for Deaf-Mutes.

Thomas's experience as a teacher, however, only reinforced his desire to be ordained. He began a program of theological study and in 1850, though remaining on the staff at the New York school, was ordained as a deacon in the Episcopal Church. In the following year, he was ordained to the priesthood.

Thomas found that his ordination opened up for him a whole new dimension to the relationships that he as a teacher had with the students at the New York Institution. When, for example, a young student named Cornelia Lathrop contracted what was to be a fatal case of tuberculosis, he was able to provide support and assistance that went far beyond the instruction that he had been able to give in the classroom. He prayed with her, gave her communion, and talked with her about her fear of death. When she died, he presided at a signed burial service that supported the deaf community in its grief.

The experience convinced Thomas that a church that incorporated the current advances in teaching for the deaf into its worship could have a powerful pastoral influence. He believed that the Episcopal Church with its fixed liturgy was particularly well suited to embark upon such a ministry. In October of 1852 he began to hold regular worship services for the deaf in a small chapel on the campus of the New York University.

The worship service was well received by New York's deaf community. Within two years the members of the congregation were formally admitted into the Annual Convention of the Diocese of New York as St. Anne's Church for the Deaf. By 1857 the congregation had outgrown the chapel in which it was meeting. It sought larger quarters, first in the New York Historical Society and then in 1859 in a building of its own. Soon the responsibility took so much of Thomas Gallaudet's time that he felt it necessary to resign from his teaching post.

Gallaudet was not content, however, to see such an effort only in one city. He began to devote a considerable portion of his time to campaigning for the creation of similar congregations in other large cities. Before 1859 was out, he had already helped establish congregations in Albany, Boston, Baltimore, Philadelphia, and Washington. Subsequent trips would take him as far as Chicago and Faribault, Minnesota.

Gallaudet could not, of course, minister to congregations in such a wide geographical area. He began, therefore, to recruit others, many of whom were themselves hearing-impaired, to join in the work. One of these was Henry Winter Syle, who, like Gallaudet, was for a time a member of the faculty of the New York Institution for Deaf-Mutes. Gallaudet enlisted Syle to teach a Bible class at St. Anne's Church. When Syle accepted a job in Philadelphia in 1874, he transferred his efforts to the deaf congregation at St. Stephen's Church in that city. Syle served as a lay reader and subsequently was ordained by the bishop of Pennsylvania as deacon (1876) and priest (1883). He was the first deaf man to enter the ordained ministry of the Episcopal Church.

Otto Berg's A Missionary Chronicle *(Hollywood, MD: St. Mary's Press, 1984) records the stories of Gallaudet, Syle, and many of the others who made the Episcopal Church a leader in the ministry to the deaf.*

Jeptha's Vow

On a warm summer day in 1854, the Reverend William Augustus Muhlenberg (1796-1876) climbed into the pulpit at St. Paul's, College Point, New York. Few would have envied his task that Sunday. The Old Testament lesson was a preacher's nightmare, the story of Jephtha's vow. Jephtha was the Gileadite general in Judges 11 who led the Israelites into battle against the Ammonites. Jephtha prayed before he went into battle, promising that if God gave him victory he would sacrifice the first person to greet him on his return home. He subdued the Ammonites and headed home to fulfill his vow. When his daughter met him with song and dance to celebrate his victory, he told her of his promise. She responded, "My father, if thou hast opened thy mouth unto the Lord, do to me according to that which hath proceeded out of thy mouth. . . . [But] let this thing be done for me: let me alone two months, that I may go up and down upon the mountains, and bewail my virginity, I and my fellows" (Judges 11:36-37).

The text was a difficult one, but Muhlenberg was committed to the lectionary. He sought to deal with the text by focusing his remarks on Jephtha's daughter, rather than centering on the curious behavior of the father in the story. He portrayed her as one who accepted a vow made to God and agreed even to forego normal family life in order to keep it. As one who was never himself to marry, Muhlenberg asked his congregation if there were modern-day Jephtha's daughters who could dedicate themselves with equal singleness of mind to the Lord.

Muhlenberg, of course, was not advocating a return to child sacrifice. Rather, he was wondering out loud whether American Episcopalians might join in the revival of the female diaconate and female monasticism that was taking place in Europe. On vacation in England in 1843, Muhlenberg heard from others about the reestablishment of the female diaconate in the Lutheran Church in Kaiserswerth, Germany, in 1836 (see pages 78-79). He also met Oxford theologian Edward Bouverie Pusey (1800-82), who at the time of Muhlenberg's visit was encouraging the efforts of a young woman to begin an order of Anglican nuns. (Sixteenth-century Anglicans had eliminated monasticism for both men and women as part of their theological reform.) Her name was Marion Hughes; she made her own monastic vows in 1841 and within four years had persuaded several others to join with her to form the Park Village Sisterhood. Muhlenberg undoubtedly had these European examples in mind when he prepared his sermon.

In many ways the sermon was not a remarkable one. Yet it deeply touched one who listened and through her became the occasion for an important transformation in the life of the church. That listener was a young woman from England named Anne Ayres (1816-96). She had immigrated to the United States in 1836 and settled in New York City, where she supported herself as a private tutor. Among her employers was Muhlenberg's sister, Mary A. Rogers. It was with Mrs. Rogers, an active Episcopal laywoman and philanthropist, that Miss Ayres had come to church that Sunday. Inspired by Muhlenberg's comments on Jephtha's daughter, she decided that she wanted to dedicate herself to the Lord's work. Muhlenberg offered his support and the two formed what was to be a lifelong friendship.

On All Saints' Day of the same year, Muhlenberg admitted Anne Ayres to what would become the Sisterhood of the Holy Communion. Like Marion Hughes before her in England, Ayres spent her initial years as the sole member of the order. Others joined her, beginning in 1853.

Ayres learned of both the Kaiserswerth deaconesses and of Hughes's Park Village Sisterhood. Others whom she influenced would separate the two institutions—the female diaconate and female monasticism— along clearer lines. Ayres, however, tried to adopt a pattern throughout her life that combined elements of both. She referred to herself as a sister but asked those who joined her sisterhood to take renewable three-year vows, rather than the life vows of nuns. She wanted the company of others but opposed any communal prayers other than the regularly scheduled services in Muhlenberg's parish.

Like both the Kaiserswerth deaconesses and many of the English sisters, Ayres devoted most of her time to medical care. When Muhlenberg's parish opened St. Luke's Episcopal Hospital in New York, Ayres became supervisor of nursing. She remained at the hospital until 1877, a year in which she transferred her efforts to St. Johnland, another Muhlenberg project that incorporated an orphanage, a school, and a retirement facility."

By the time of Ayres's death in 1896, both the female diaconate and female monasticism were firmly established in the Episcopal Church in the United States. The 1890 *Church Almanac* listed the names of twenty-one sisterhoods. The New York Training School for Deaconesses and the Church Training and Deaconesses House of the Diocese of Pennsylvania, both of which opened in 1891, prepared an increasing number of women for ministry in the church; the 1909 *Church Almanac*, the first to provide statistics, recorded the names of 143 active deaconesses.

Ayres recorded her reaction to the sermon on Jephtha's vow in her biography of Muhlenberg. It is reprinted in Readings from the History of the Episcopal Church *(Wilton, CT: Morehouse Publishing, 1986).*

St. Andrew's Infirmary

The Reverend and Mrs. Horace Stringfellow of Baltimore, Maryland, wanted a hospital. They had come to Baltimore in 1853 when Mr. Stringfellow had accepted a call to St. Andrew's Church. Both Stringfellows strongly believed that the responsibility of the church was not limited to those who attended worship; it was their conviction that the church should care for all needy persons in the area in which it was situated. The needs of the inhabitants of St. Andrew's neighborhood were manifold. Unemployment was high, and salaries were low. Educational opportunities for children were limited. But the Stringfellows were particularly concerned about the poor medical care. The area lacked a proper medical facility, and as time passed, they became increasingly convinced that they were the ones to begin it.

Mr. Stringfellow took an extended tour of England in 1855 in the hope that he might improve his health, which had been badly weakened by constant demands of his ministry. Yet even in Europe, he did not stop thinking about the needs of the people at home. Indeed, he turned his tour in England into a fact-finding trip. He suspected that the only way to begin a hospital with his limited resources would be to secure the cooperation of deaconesses who would be willing to serve without salary. He visited, therefore, orphanages run by English deaconesses and schools run by French nuns. He read about Pastor Fliedner and the Lutheran deaconesses at Kaiserswerth in Germany. He talked with the bishop of Oxford about efforts within his diocese. He spoke at length with William Augustus Muhlenberg, who was also on tour in England at the same time. Muhlenberg told of Anne Ayres's Sisterhood of the Holy Communion in New York.

On his return from Europe, Mr. Stringfellow was ready to put his newly found information to work. He spoke with his wife about setting aside deaconesses to work in the parish. When she gave her hearty agreement, he corresponded with Bishop William Whittingham. Whittingham gave his consent, and the Stringfellows began to circulate word of their plan throughout the diocese.

A Miss Mary Black and a Miss Catherine Minard were the first women to express interest in the project. The Stringfellows were disappointed at first. Mr. Stringfellow had only a salary of $1,400 a year with which to support a family of five; he had hoped to attract candidates with some independent income of their own to contribute to the project. Misses Black and Minard had no funds, but they were deeply interested in serving in the diaconate. The Stringfellows decided, therefore, to go ahead with plans.

After a service of dedication, deaconesses Black and Minard moved into the rectory with the Stringfellows and their three children. The women visited homes in the neighborhood during the day, providing some basic medical advice and nursing care. At 6:00 P.M. each evening, they held "office hours" in the front hall of the rectory. As many as thirty people would come each evening to seek the women's advice and assistance.

When the two additional mouths put too much strain on the food budget, Mrs. Stringfellow opened a private school in order to supplement the family income. When it became obvious that the deaconesses needed more space in which to work, the Stringfellows located a more suitable building. When Mr. Stringfellow's initial efforts to find a woman to serve as the administrator of the new building proved unsuccessful, the Stringfellows themselves planned to move in to serve in that capacity. A Mrs. Lyle learned of and expressed interest in the facility, however, and by 1856 the women had moved to the new location, which they named the St. Andrew's Infirmary.

Before the year was out, the Stringfellows were ready to move to another parish. Mr. Stringfellow accepted a call to St. James Church in Hyde Park, New York. In their few years in Baltimore, however, the Stringfellows had left a permanent mark on the life of the church. Ten years earlier Anne Ayres of New York had entered a parish sisterhood that combined elements of both the Kaiserswerth diaconate for women and the English renewal of women's monasticism. The order that the Stringfellows planned was, however, clearly an order of deaconesses. It was perhaps the first explicit order of deaconesses in the American Episcopal Church.

The deaconesses left their own mark on the Stringfellow family. Deaconess Minard and Deaconess Black nursed the Stringfellow's young son in the final stages of a fatal illness. Indeed, the Stringfellow's dying child was the deaconesses' first patient. It was in their care of him that the sisters first sharpened the healing skills with which they would later serve many others.

The Bat and the Bishop

Clerical and lay delegates from the Diocese of New Jersey met in 1859 to elect a bishop. George Washington Doane, who as bishop had guided the diocese with a strong hand for twenty-seven years, had died. Few who attended the election expected it to be a difficult choice. Milo Mahan was the clear favorite of the clergy. Moreover, Bishop Doane had given approval of Mahan from his deathbed.

Born in Suffolk, Virginia, in 1819, Mahan had attended William A. Muhlenberg's St. Paul's Academy in Flushing, New York. He was an excellent student and at the age of seventeen was chosen to teach Greek at the Episcopal High School in Alexandria, Virginia. After six or seven years, however, Mahan became involved in a dispute with Bishop William Meade and resigned. Mahan, it seemed, showed more interest in the catholic theological revival that had begun among Anglican clergy at Oxford in 1833 than the good bishop thought prudent. By one account Meade found a copy of the Oxford theologians' *Tracts for the Times* on Mahan's bookshelf and fired him on the spot.

Mahan returned to New York to teach at St. Paul's. His career prospered. Within ten years he entered the ordained ministry, published a book on theology, became editor of the *Church Journal*, and accepted a position on the faculty of General Seminary.

Mahan's position, professor of ecclesiastical history, was a particularly important one. In the pecking order of the nineteenth-century Episcopal seminaries, the professor of ecclesiastical history was the heir apparent to the professor of systematic divinity. It was a position that boards of trustees awarded to promising young scholars whom they hoped would become leading theologians in the church. A priest in such a position, moreover, would also be a strong candidate for election as bishop. Two of Mahan's predecessors, Benjamin T. Onderdonk and William R. Whittingham, had already been elected to the episcopate.

Those who planned the New Jersey convention were certain that Mahan would be elected. They even invited him to preach at the opening service. In the midst of this service, however, something happened that changed the minds of a number of those present.

As Mahan mounted the pulpit, a bat appeared and circled him several times, finally striking him full in the face. No one had ever witnessed such a failure in navigation on the part of a bat. Some superstitiously saw it as a sign that Mahan would not make a suitable bishop. In the balloting that followed, Mahan received strong support on twelve consecutive ballots, but was never able to secure a majority in both orders. In the end, the clergy and laity elected Philadelphia priest William H. Odenheimer as a compromise candidate.

Mahan remained at General for several more years before accepting a parish position in Baltimore. As a Southerner he found life in New York uncomfortable during the Civil War. After the war he was elected to the chair of systematic divinity at General. He would never, however, be elected a bishop.

In 1875 John Henry Hopkins, Jr., edited a three-volume Collected Works of Mahan. *Hopkins, best known for his authorship of "We Three Kings," included a memoir in the first volume.*

Enmegahbowh

In fall of 1859, newly consecrated missionary Bishop Henry Benjamin Whipple headed for the Diocese of Minnesota. Minnesota was new both as a diocese and as a state. The state joined the union in 1858. General Convention created the diocese in 1857 and elected Whipple as its first bishop two years later.

To some in the church, Whipple seemed ill-prepared for his new responsibility. The new bishop had never served in the diocese over which he was elected to preside. He had spent his relatively brief ordained ministry in the state of New York (1849-57) and in Chicago, Illinois (1857-59). Like most western missionary bishops, he was also relatively young. He was only thirty-seven at the time of his election.

Whipple's fellow Episcopalians offered him their advice. On many matters the content of their counsel to him differed. On one matter, however—the church's ministry to Native Americans—most agreed. Whipple later recollected in his autobiography: "Good men advised me to have nothing to do with Indian Missions, on the ground that the red men were a degraded, perishing race" (Henry Benjamin Whipple, *Lights and Shadows of a Long Episcopate* [New York: Macmillan, 1899], p. 32). Whipple's advisors apparently felt that Native Americans were the people of the past and that the Episcopal Church should concentrate on the European immigrants who held the promise of the future. Many in Whipple's circumstance would have accepted the advice. A friendship early in Whipple's episcopate, however, convinced him otherwise.

While Whipple was the first missionary bishop of Minnesota, he was not the first Episcopal clergyman to visit the area. Prior to its creation as a diocese, Minnesota had been part of the large seven-state territory over which Jackson Kemper, the Episcopal Church's first missionary bishop, presided. Kemper had been able to visit the territory and had been able to convince a few clergymen to serve there in missions.

One of these was Enmegahbowh, an Ottawa Indian, who had been raised as a Christian in Canada. As a boy he had lived with the family of an Anglican clergyman who had persuaded him to learn English. Later he served in western Canada as an interpreter for Methodist missionaries and as a school teacher. While on tour with Methodist missionaries in Minnesota, however, he met and married a young Indian woman, who later took the Christian name Charlotte. The missionaries returned to Canada, but Enmegahbowh remained in Minnesota with his new wife. He feared, at first, that he had lost contact with other Christians and at one point planned to return to Canada despite his promise to Charlotte's parents that he would remain in Minnesota. The arrival of Episcopal missionaries ended his dilemma, however, and he soon cooperated in their efforts. Bishop Kemper recognized the value of Enmegahbowh for Indian missions and designated him as a lay reader. In 1859 he ordained him a deacon. At the time that Whipple arrived in Minnesota, Enmegahbowh was serving at St. Columba's, Gull Lake, a seven-year-old Ojibway congregation.

Bishop Whipple visited St. Columba's during his first month in the diocese. He was deeply impressed by the Indian deacon and took an instant liking to him. The two became fast friends. Thereafter, Enmegahbowh often accompanied the bishop on his visitations of the diocese. The Indian served as interpreter and guide. His hunting ability often provided the bishop with the food they ate during the travels. In time, he also became a leading fund-raiser for the diocese, visiting the East in order to secure financial support.

Soon after meeting the Indian deacon, Whipple had made a pledge about his episcopate. "I knew," he later wrote, "all that men could tell me of difficulty and danger, but when I bowed my head at the foot of the cross I believed that there was room for all men, and that if it were dark in the Indian country it was light above. I resolved that, God being my helper, it should never be said that the first Bishop of Minnesota turned his back upon" the Indians (Whipple, *Lights and Shadows*, p. 32). With Enmegahbowh's help, Whipple was good to his word. By the end of his long episcopate, Whipple's fellow Episcopalians called him the "Apostle to the Red Men." His example inspired others to emulate his work in the territories farther west. To this day the only areas of the country in which the Episcopal church is numerically the largest denomination are in Indian reservations.

The Ecclesiastical Career of John Henry Hopkins

At the time of his death in 1868, John Henry Hopkins of Vermont was one of the most distinguished bishops in all of the Anglican Communion. As a priest, he had twice represented the Diocese of Pennsylvania in General Convention. As a bishop, he had served the Diocese of Vermont for thirty-six years and the national church as presiding bishop for thirteen. He had been chosen the professor of theology for a school planned in Massachusetts and had been given two honorary degrees. He had published verse, had written the first American work on gothic architecture, and had drafted the initial site plans for the University of the South. He was the most prolific author in the House of Bishops with more than a dozen works on theological topics. His 1851 letter to the archbishop of Canterbury was one of the elements that led to the calling of the first Lambeth Conference (1868), a gathering in which he played a prominent role.

Anyone examining his long and distinguished record in 1868 might well have imagined an auspicious beginning of such an ordained ministry. One could well construct a promising career as a student at one of the country's finer colleges, an intense period of postgraduate study in one of the Episcopal Church's new theological seminaries, and an apprenticeship as the assistant of a wise and experienced priest. The reality had been, however, quite different.

He was, for example, a graduate of neither a college nor a seminary. His parents, who had emigrated from Ireland when he was eight, had been able to pay for two years of study at a Baptist boarding school, but a college education was beyond their means. Hopkins had, therefore, halted his education at fifteen and entered a Philadelphia counting house. He had no further formal education, though in his midtwenties he did read for the law with a Pittsburgh attorney. (He was admitted to the bar in 1818.) All the remainder of Hopkins's education was the result of individual study or the instruction of his parents.

Hopkins's entrance into the ordained ministry was also somewhat irregular. Indeed, had it not been for a chance remark, he might not have entered the ordained ministry at all. He made the remark in the spring of 1822 to a fellow member of Trinity Episcopal Church in Pittsburgh. Hopkins was at the time a fairly successful lawyer with a happy marriage and a growing family. He confided to a friend, however, that he was troubled. His wife's brother, a handsome and popular young man who was engaged to be married, had been injured in a carriage accident and had died soon afterward. Hopkins, shaken by the death, began to examine his own life and priorities. Should he, he asked aloud, have entered the ordained ministry rather than the law? With the passage of time, however, his anxiety decreased, and he decided that he had chosen the right course. The friend, however, did not forget the remark.

In July of the following year the rector of Trinity Church resigned, and the vestry of which both Hopkins and his friend were members convened in order to seek a replacement. Hopkins was away on business at the time of the meeting, but his friend was not. When the vestry had exhausted possible candidates for rector without reaching an agreement, the friend nominated Hopkins.

Others on the vestry raised immediate objections. Hopkins was not a priest. He had, moreover, an occupation that paid considerably more than the position of rector. Yet the friend persisted. In the end the vestry elected Hopkins as rector of the parish.

On his return to Pittsburgh, Hopkins was startled to learn that he was the unanimous choice of his fellow vestry members for rector. He questioned the decision, citing the financial loss to his family, the inconvenience to his clients, and his lack of qualifications. His circle of friends prevailed upon him, however. He agreed and in September wrote to the bishop of Pennsylvania for advice. The bishop acted swiftly. He prescribed a course of study and within nine months had ordained him a deacon (December 1823) and priest (May 1824).

Despite his limited education and the irregular path by which he entered the priesthood, Hopkins soon demonstrated that he had a brilliant mind and a gift for theological discourse. His colleagues in the Episcopal Church recognized those gifts. Within two years of his ordination to the priesthood they elected him a deputy to General Convention; within three, they advanced his name as a leading candidate for bishop of Pennsylvania; within nine, they elected him bishop of Vermont.

McIlvaine Preserves the Church

In the years following the close of the Civil War, Bishop Charles Pettit McIlvaine found himself in an unfamiliar position. Quick-witted and outspoken, the bishop had always been a gadfly, a strong critic of what he saw as excess and error in the church. Now in his later years, he found himself in the role of mediator and moderate.

In the first decades of the century, McIlvaine had been one of the "District Clergy," a group of young clergymen who had congregated in the area of the nation's capital. They shared certain convictions, the foremost of which was a belief that Episcopalians should emphasize personal faith and piety, and they soon provided the core for what became known as the evangelical party. Like their counterparts—New York City's high-church Episcopalians, who emphasized the denomination's apostolic succession—the District Clergy were extremely influential in shaping the nineteenth-century Episcopal Church. Within a matter of years they founded a theological seminary (Virginia), published a theological journal (*The Washington Theological Repertory*), reversed the outcome of an election of a bishop (the election of a successor for James Madison of Virginia), and had one of their number (William H. Wilmer) elected president of William and Mary College.

Like others in the group, McIlvaine advanced rapidly in the church hierarchy. The son of a New Jersey senator, he was appointed chaplain at West Point in 1825. While there, he proved so successful in promoting personal religion among the students that some critics complained that he would sap the zeal of America's future fighting men. From West Point he moved to St. Anne's Brooklyn. In 1832, at the age of thirty-three, he was elected the second bishop of Ohio.

The diocese had a college and a seminary. These McIlvaine soon brought into agreement with his views. When, for example, news of the Oxford movement reached America, the bishop wrote a theological critique and required its use as a text at the seminary. Within the House of Bishops, he was equally partisan. He worked for the trial of three high-church bishops (of whom two were convicted), and he played an important role in the interrogation of the faculty of General Seminary.

High-church and evangelical skirmishes were temporarily halted by the Civil War, but when the war ended the dispute began anew. The debate soon centered around the word *regeneration*. In the language of the prayer book, regeneration referred to the change in condition resulting from baptism. As most Episcopalians understood this change before the Oxford movement, one was offered a covenant relationship with God in baptism in which salvation was possible on the conditions of repentance and faith. In the common language of most American Protestants, however, regeneration referred to the mature adult decision to exercise the terms of the covenant, a decision that could accompany a dramatic emotional conversion. So long as most American Protestants agreed that both the baptism and the adult acceptance were necessary, the conflicting use of the word *regeneration* caused no serious problems. When Oxford theologians began to suggest, however, that no specific point of acceptance of the covenant existed other than baptism, Episcopalians began to quarrel about language. Evangelicals suggested that the church drop the word *regeneration* from the baptismal office and follow the general Protestant usage. High-church Episcopalians, reserving judgment for a time on the merits of the Oxford argument, opposed the alteration in language, fearing that such a change would be a surrender of their church's central principles.

In 1869 an evangelical parish priest in Illinois, Charles E. Cheney, began to omit the word *regeneration* from the baptismal service without awaiting the action of the General Convention. His bishop brought him to trial; he would ultimately be deprived of his orders. Evangelicals came rapidly to Cheney's defense, signing petitions on his behalf.

McIlvaine was faced with a difficult decision. He was the only surviving member of the District Clergy in the House of Bishops.

Not only the senior figure in the evangelical movement, he was also a respected bishop and theological author. Would he lend his authority to the Cheney protest?

Yet he sensed danger. Many of the younger evangelicals placed party spirit ahead of any commitment to their denomination as a whole. They had begun to talk of schism and new denominations. By siding with them, McIlvaine could certainly capture an important following, but it might be at the expense of destroying the church.

McIlvaine chose the unaccustomed role of moderate. He put the interest of the denomination as a whole before his personal and party preferences. While he was uncomfortable with the word *regeneration*, he supported the decisions of the General Convention. He soon penned a circular letter to evangelicals calling for them to avoid precipitous action and to await the 1871 Convention. He asked his assistant bishop to seek supporting signatures from other evangelical leaders. He worked through proper channels to seek a change in the language of the prayer book, and when it became evident that the effort would fail, he worked out another compromise. The House of Bishops declared, with only one dissenting vote, that baptismal regeneration did not include the "moral change" that took place in the adult Christian who exercised the provisions of the covenant. Following the Convention, McIlvaine defended the compromise, calling it "the best thing yet." When his own seminary professors expressed some doubts about the precise language of the statement, he fired the entire faculty.

So long as McIlvaine lived there would be no schism in the Episcopal Church. He held the evangelical wing in the denomination in the troubled year of 1871. He had checked the momentum for division. When, after his death in 1873, a group did leave to form the Reformed Episcopal Church, their number would be small, involving only a limited percentage of evangelical parishes. McIlvaine, the unlikely moderate, had helped to preserve the church he so loved.

Oakerhater and Alice Pendleton

In 1875, Alice Pendleton was able to spend a much needed winter vacation in Florida. At the time, her busy husband, George Hunt Pendleton, did not hold any of the public offices that marked his adult career. By 1875 he had already served in the Ohio Senate (1854-56), in the U.S. House of Representatives (1857-65), and on the federal bench. After running unsuccessfully for vice president (1864) and governor of Ohio (1869), he temporarily retired from public life. He would serve as the president of the Kentucky Central Railroad for ten years before election to the U.S. Senate in 1879. The demands of the railway presidency were apparently light enough to allow the Pendletons the opportunity to spend a winter in St. Augustine, Florida.

Mrs. Pendleton enjoyed the vacation, but she was not content simply to sit in the sun. With an active mind and a particular interest in public affairs, she carefully followed national events. When the federal government decided to confine twenty-eight Native Americans at the Fort Marion Military Prison on St. Augustine, she went to investigate. Her interest may have simply been aroused by local publicity surrounding the transfer of the men to the prison. It was equally possible, however, that her interest in Native Americans was of longer standing. During her youth, her father, Francis Scott Key, had served as President Jackson's envoy in negotiations about the Creek Indians with the state of Alabama.

The men who were imprisoned were Cheyenne Indians who had participated in the Battle of Adobe Walls in 1874 and in a series of skirmishes in the following year. Mrs. Pendleton was able to convince the military authorities to allow her to visit some of them. She soon made friends with four of the prisoners. Meeting with them regularly, she turned conversation to matters of religion. All four embraced the Christian faith. Anxious to share with others of their race the good news that they had received, the four began to express interest in the ordained ministry.

Mrs. Pendleton was supportive of their plans. Joining forces with Deaconess Mary Burnham, who learned of the Indians while on a visit to her brother in St. Augustine in 1878, she campaigned successfully for their release from prison. With money raised by Mrs. Pendleton, the four Indians traveled to Central New York (Deaconess Burnham's diocese), where the Episcopal Church had the longest continuous experience with ministry among Native Americans. They studied with an Episcopal priest who shared their interest in evangelism.

In 1881, one of the group, Oakerhater, was ordained a deacon. He journeyed to the Indian Territory (Oklahoma) in the company of the priest from New York with whom he had studied. The priest returned to New York in 1884, but Oakerhater continued his ministry at Cheyenne Agency at Darlington and later at the Whirlwind Episcopal Mission.

Oakerhater was not the first Native American deacon in the Episcopal Church. He was never advanced by his bishop to the priesthood, yet he would provide so striking a model of faithful service during thirty-six years of full-time ministry and fifteen years of active retirement that the 1985 General Convention added his name to the Episcopal Church's calendar.

Oakerhater was the first to preach about the faith in Christ to many of the Cheyenne. He never forgot the difference that the witness of one other person had made in his life. Indeed, from the day of his baptism, he carried a perpetual reminder of that witness. For, following the custom of many nineteenth-century Episcopalians who were baptized as adults, he chose a new name at his baptism—David *Pendleton* Oakerhater.

The United Thank Offering

In 1885 two Episcopalians who were deeply involved in missions were locked in an institutional power struggle. One was Mary Abbot Twing of the Woman's Auxiliary to the Board of Missions (general secretary, 1872-76; honorary secretary since 1883). The second was the Reverend William S. Langford, the newly appointed general secretary of the mission board's Board of Managers. Their dispute was about money. Local and diocesan women's groups were becoming increasingly effective in raising funds for domestic and foreign missions. Some of the money that they raised was contributed to the Board of Missions; other gifts were made directly to specific missionary projects. Mrs. Twing felt that the women's groups had the right to designate how their funds were to be spent. The Reverend Mr. Langford disagreed; he felt that the elected (male) officers of the Board of Missions should have the final say about the allocation of all funds.

The Reverend Mr. Langford made the first move. He convinced the managers of the Board of Missions that a constitutional provision was needed to define the proper relationship of the Woman's Auxiliary to the Board of Missions. It was difficult, he reasoned, for the board to adopt a comprehensive plan for missions if women's auxiliaries continued to designate their funds to individual pet projects. A new constitution could make it clear that the auxiliaries were to contribute to the board's treasury. The managers agreed to take the matter to the full board membership at a meeting scheduled for the following year.

Mrs. Twing responded with a plan of her own. The women's auxiliaries, she suggested, did not need to be more closely defined as dependencies of the Board of Missions. They needed a more extensive organization that would incorporate, not only women's efforts in support of missions, but all activity by women in the church. As the first nationwide Episcopal women's organization, the Woman's Auxiliary to the Board of Missions would be the appropriate place to begin work on such a plan. Rather than limiting the autonomy of female Episcopalians, the Board of Missions should expand it.

Faced with the strong personalities of Mr. Langford and Mrs. Twing, the members of the board decided that discretion was the better part of valor. Rather than supporting either of the two proposals, they chose to take no action at all.

Mrs. Twing had won the skirmish. She became convinced, nonetheless, that Episcopal women needed a mechanism to allocate funds on a national level. Mrs. Ida Soule, a friend of Mrs. Twing and a delegate to the session of the Woman's Auxiliary that met at the time of the 1886 General Convention, suggested that women would contribute more to the offering collected during their meeting if they knew the objects for which their funds were to be used. The General Convention of 1889 approved the creation of a United (Thank) Offering to be both supported by and allocated by women. Armed with this new budgetary device, the Woman's Auxiliary was able to funnel funds to projects that were supported by and beneficial to women. Between 1898 and 1910, the offering would support the salaries of almost 1,500 women workers. In more recent years, as the male monopoly on leadership positions in the church has come to an end, the United Thank Offering has widened its goals, no longer focusing only on projects that benefit women. Contributors are no longer only females. One essential element has, however, remained the same. Women decide how the funds are to be spent. Mrs. Twing would have approved.

Mary Sudman Donovan's A Different Call *(Wilton, CT: Morehouse Publishing, 1986) tells the story of Mrs. Twing and other female leaders in the Episcopal Church in the period between 1850 and 1920.*

Huntington's Quadrilateral

For almost a century after the formation of the Protestant Episcopal Church in 1789, American Episcopalians carried on an internal debate that made ecumenical relationships with other Protestants virtually impossible. By the middle of the nineteenth century many of the better minds in the church bemoaned the continuing dispute and sought ways around it. It would not be, however, until the thirty-fifth General Convention in 1886 that an Episcopalian offered a reasonable solution to the difficulty. The one who did so was William Reed Huntington (1838-1909). His solution opened the doors to the rich ecumenical activities of the Episcopal Church in the twentieth century.

The continuing debate among Episcopalians was about covenant theology and episcopacy. Seventeenth-century Protestants used the biblical idea of covenant to explain the necessity of Christian morality. While it was true that God saved the sinner who believed in Christ without reference to that sinner's own works (the Reformation doctrine of justification by faith alone), it was also true that God entered into a covenant relationship with the justified person. When Christians fulfilled their part of the covenant (by faith and repentance), God responded with forgiveness and eternal life. The concept of the covenant thus allowed Protestant theologians to assert two initially contradictory propositions: God saved without reference to works (God chose to whom to offer the covenant); and God expected good works from sinners (in order to fulfill their covenant requirements).

Seventeenth-century Anglican covenant theologians often developed the covenant argument with two additions. They identified baptism as the office through which one was admitted to the covenant relationship, and they suggested—in opposition to Presbyterians, Congregationalists, and others who would have eliminated the office of bishop—that such a baptism was not valid unless conveyed by a priest ordained in apostolic succession. Such a provision made little difference for those within the Anglican Church, for they already enjoyed an apostolic ministry. It made a great deal of difference, however, in ecumenical relations. For those who accepted the additions to the covenant argument, other Protestants were simply not part of the covenant.

Thomas Bray (1656-1739), the founder of the missionary society that provided the American colonies with the majority of their clergy in the eighteenth century, was one of many who incorporated this argument into his writings. American Anglicans learned of the importance of episcopacy for the covenant from the widely read commentary on the catechism that Bray prepared. Particularly in New England where Congregationalists looked down upon them as a poorer group of more recent immigrants whose theology was suspect, Anglicans found solace in the covenant argument. By the time of the formation of the American church in 1789, most New England Episcopalians and a significant percentage of those in other states subscribed to the theory.

Quite naturally, those who adhered to the argument refused any cooperation with other Protestants. Bishop John Henry Hobart (1775-1830) of New York, for example, refused to allow clergy of his diocese to participate in the American Bible Society. Individual Episcopal clergymen and congregations participated in ecumenical endeavors, but Hobart and other advocates of the apostolic orders-covenant theology successfully prevented the denomination as a whole from entering into any ecumenical discussions with other Protestants. They refused to participate with those who were not part of the Christian covenant.

William Reed Huntington, an active member of the House of Deputies from 1871 until 1907, was well aware of this objection as he prepared for the General Convention of 1886. He had, however, a possible solution. What if the Episcopal Church went on record as declaring its strong convictions on both the desirability of ecumenical discussion and the necessity of the episcopacy? Perhaps such an explicit declaration could calm the fears of those advocates of the apostolic orders-covenant theology who worried that ecumenical discussion might lead to an abandoning of the apostolic succession. Ecumenical discussion might become the very means of granting apostolic succession to the denominations that lacked it.

Huntington prepared a *quadrilateral* (a four-part statement) in which he identified four essential elements for the restoration of the unity of the church: the Holy Scriptures, the Nicene Creed, the two great sacraments (baptism and eucharist), and the historic episcopate. Episcopalians wanted, Huntington suggested, to cooperate with those who accepted this common faith and order so "to discount schism, to heal the wounds of the Body of Christ, and to promote the charity which is the chief of Christian graces and the visible manifestation of Christ to the world."

The House of Bishops not only adopted the quadrilateral but also forwarded the statement to the international gathering of Anglican bishops at the Lambeth Conference that met two years later. The conference endorsed the document.

Armed with the newly adopted Chicago-Lambeth Quadrilateral, Episcopalians entered the twentieth century with a new sense of ecumenical responsibility. In particular, Charles Henry Brent (1862-1929) helped work out the implications of such a statement for the Episcopal Church. An active voice for Christian unity, he chaired the first World Conference on Faith and Order in 1927. The Faith and Order Conference would merge in 1948 with several other bodies that promoted Christian unity in order to form the World Council of Churches.

Huntington's simple statement that proved so productive of ecumenical relationships is printed in the historical documents section of the 1979 Book of Common Prayer *on pages 876-78.*

The Proposed Book and the Book Annexed

Most Episcopalians are aware that the current *Book of Common Prayer* is one in a series of American prayer books that stretches back to the years immediately after the American Revolution. They know that the General Convention of 1789 adopted the first American prayer book as a replacement for the British 1662 *Book of Common Prayer* and that subsequent American Conventions adopted the prayer books of 1892, 1928, and 1979. Few Episcopalians realize, however, that the process of liturgical revisions has also had dead ends. The bishops and deputies at General Convention rejected two revisions of the prayer book.

The first failure was the product of the 1785 General Convention. Deputies from seven middle-Atlantic and Southern states (North Carolina and Georgia were not represented) drafted a *Proposed Book* for use in the American church. Their task was a difficult one, and they were not entirely successful. The priests and laypersons who attended the Convention hoped to please three different groups: the parishioners of the middle-Atlantic and Southern states that they represented; the clergy and laity of the four New England and two Southern states that did not participate; and the British archbishops who they hoped would consecrate bishops for their fledgling organization. Within eight months the clear verdict was in. While all agreed a new book was needed—Americans could not, for example, continue to pray that King George III would defeat all his enemies—many of those that the participants in the Convention had hoped to please complained that the changes in the *Proposed Book* were too sweeping. The book, for example, omitted the Nicene Creed and decreased the number of the Thirty-nine Articles to twenty.

The clergy and laity who assembled in the following year for the next General Convention reversed their previous action and rejected the *Proposed Book*. In 1789 they adopted a revision that incorporated fewer changes from the English prayer book than had the 1785 liturgy.

The second failure was the *Book Annexed*. A joint committee of the House of Bishops and House of Deputies, which had been appointed in 1880, reported to the General Convention of 1883. The committee members made their presentation in two ways. They drafted an intricate fifty-page resolution detailing the specific changes that they advocated, and they appended a sample prayer book— the *Book Annexed*—to the report.

The committee was an impressive body of twenty-one that included John Williams (bishop of Connecticut, and later presiding bishop), Morgan Dix (rector of the Trinity Church, New York, and president of the House of Deputies from 1886 to 1898), William Reed Huntington (author of the Chicago-Lambeth Quadrilateral), Hugh Sheffey (speaker of the Virginia House of Deputies), and Hamilton Fish (former New York governor and U.S. Secretary of State). Well aware of the ways that their nation had grown since the 1780s, they were anxious to prepare a revision that was relevant to American life. Two examples were indicative of their sentiments. They created a "Short Office of Prayer for Sundry Occasions" so that parish clergy could provide brief noonday services for city workers on lunch hour; and they added additional prayers that took America's growing industry into account. A General Intercession drafted by committee members included these petitions:

> Be merciful to all whose duties are difficult or burdensome, and comfort them concerning their toil. Shield from bodily accident and harm the workmen at their work. Protect the efforts of sober and honest industry, and suffer not the hire of labourers to be kept back by fraud. Incline the hearts of employers and of those whom they employ to mutual forbearance, fairness, and goodwill. (*Book Annexed*, p. 49)

The bishops and deputies at the 1883 convention were impressed with the *Book Annexed*. They made some minor modifications but accepted most of the proposals. Since the canons of the church required the approval of two consecutive Conventions for the adoption of a new prayer book, the presiding bishop and the president of the House of Deputies reappointed the committee members and instructed them to present the modified form of the *Book Annexed* to the Convention of 1886.

In the interim between Conventions, a number of Episcopalians began to raise objections to the *Book Annexed*. Some complained because of sectional rivalries; fifteen of the original twenty-one members of the liturgical committee were from Connecticut, New York, or Pennsylvania. Others objected that the prayer book was too ritualistic or not ritualistic enough. Still others had been caught by surprise by the whole revision process and wanted the chance to leave their mark on the end product.

Fearing defeat of the modified *Book Annexed*, committee members adopted an elaborate strategy. They divided the changes in the book into three categories. They collected the one-third that they regarded as most popular into "schedule A" and submitted it for approval on second reading. They revised another third of the material and prepared a "schedule B"; since this material would only have the approval of one Convention, it would need to be resubmitted to the 1889 Convention. They proposed putting the final third, which contained the most innovative material, into a separate volume to be called the *Book of Offices*.

The committee's strategy proved too intricate. A deputies committee ruled that the church's constitution did not allow for a *Book of Offices*. (The idea did not die, however. The General Convention did finally approve a book by that name in 1937.) The deputies and bishops also found that they ran out of time. When the session ended, they still had not acted on half of the resolutions of schedule B.

The members of the convention were so confused that they would need two further sessions—1889 and 1892—to complete the process of revision. The end product—the *Book of Common Prayer* 1892—was an unhappy compromise that lacked the innovative aspects and the deep social concern of the *Book Annexed*. Within twenty years, bishops and deputies were already engaged in the revision process that eventually produced the 1928 prayer book. It would not be until 1979, however, that the General Convention would adopt a prayer book edition that captured the more innovative aspects of the *Book Annexed*.

Neve's Dream

In 1888, Frederick William Neve was elected rector of Emmanuel, Greenwood and St. Paul's, Ivy in Albemarle County, Virginia. Neve was an Englishman. A graduate of Oxford, he came to Virginia after seven years in English parishes. His ministry at Emmanuel was a good and joyful one that extended over seventeen years. It was, however, the work at St. Paul's that stole his heart.

As Neve ventured out of the church into the surrounding countryside, he found isolated mountain communities that lacked schools, churches, and health care. He began to dream a great dream: Could God be calling the Episcopal Church to minister to the people of the Blue Ridge? Could Episcopalians build a series of active mountain missions throughout the region in which the gospel could be preached, the sacraments celebrated, the rudiments of education given to children, and the most pressing physical needs of the people met?

It took Neve some time to convince others of the wisdom of his dream. By the turn of the century, however, he had enlisted an important ally, Bishop Robert A. Gibson (bishop coadjutor 1897-1902, bishop of Virginia 1902-19). In 1904, Bishop Gibson appointed Neve archdeacon of the Blue Ridge. The following year Neve resigned as rector of Emmanuel in order to devote himself more fully to the mountain ministry. His relationship with St. Paul's, Ivy would, however, continue for the remainder of his life. He served as rector until 1923, and, when he retired in that year and vacated the rectory, he built a home in the community.

Neve reported to the diocesan council of 1906, asking for the formation of an advisory board. With an active board and increasing financial support, Neve was able to establish a network of new missions. In 1909 it was already necessary to found a boarding school (the Blue Ridge School) to provide more advanced instruction to children who had completed their studies at mission day schools. Later a second institution would be added: St. Anne's Preventorium provided health care for those suffering from tuberculosis and malnutrition.

By the time that Neve died in 1948 at the ripe age of ninety-two, there were twenty-six missions in seven counties in the archdeaconry. Though usually small, these churches ministered to some five hundred families and approximately 1,600 communicants. There were six priests, one bishop (W. Roy Mason had succeeded Neve as archdeacon, and when he was elected suffragan in 1941, he continued to exercise supervision over the district), and twenty-five others working in the missions.

The twenty-five were laypersons and deaconesses; throughout the life of the archdeaconry, they had done the great majority of the local mission work. In the early years, most of these workers in the archdeaconry had come from outside the Blue Ridge. In time, however, many of the leaders were themselves products of mission churches. In 1948, for example, the headmaster of Blue Ridge School was a mission school graduate.

Though the archdeaconry was integrated into the diocesan structure in 1953, the Diocese of Virginia continues to be very much marked by Frederick Neve's dream. Many parishes in the diocese owe their origin to the archdeaconry (Good Shepherd, Hickory; Good Shepherd, Bluemont; Grace, Red Hill; Holy Cross, Afton; St. Andrew's, Ada; St. George's, Stanley; St. John-the-Baptist, Ivy; St. Paul's, Ingham; St. Stephen and the Good Shepherd, Rocky Bar), and many individuals still remember firsthand the work in the archdeaconry.

"Racial" Bishops and Archdeacons

A person attending the General Convention of 1916 would have heard numerous private discussions and frequent floor debates on what the Convention's bishops and deputies called the "racial episcopate." Some favored "racial" bishops, while others called for suffragans. To make sense of the issue one would have to have been acquainted with the history of the Episcopal Church in the 1880s and 1890s. The 1916 debate was in many ways the logical outgrowth of a missionary strategy adopted by many dioceses during those years.

Like many American denominations, the Episcopal Church lost a considerable percentage of its black membership following the Civil War. In the years prior to the war, slaves made up the majority of the members of the church in some Southern dioceses. In South Carolina, for example, eight times as many blacks were confirmed as whites in 1859. When the Civil War ended, however, increasing numbers of freed blacks joined all-black denominations, which guaranteed them a measure of self-determination. General Convention established a Freedman's Commission in 1865 to assist blacks in the South, and in 1878 Virginia Episcopalians opened a theological seminary for black candidates. The efforts helped decrease the rate of membership loss, but the wounds of recent slavery were too deep and the acceptance of white members too tentative to make a truly integrated church possible.

Other primarily white churches were no more effective. Among mainline hierarchical "white" Protestant denominations today, black membership ranges from approximately 1 percent in the Lutheran Church to just under 4 percent in the United Methodist Church. Approximately 5 percent of present-day Episcopalians are black. But back in the 1880s and 1890s, many Episcopalians believed that something more could be done. They were particularly aware of the need to develop black leadership in their denomination.

In 1890, Bishop Edwin G. Weed of Florida suggested one possible approach. He appointed an episcopal assistant with special responsibility for the black congregations of his diocese. Other dioceses in areas with large black populations would follow the South Carolina example by appointing what came to be called "Archdeacons for Colored Work." South Carolina appointed its first Archdeacon for Colored Work in 1892; Virginia and North Carolina followed in 1901. By 1903 the Diocese of Pennsylvania had an archdeacon working with black congregations in Philadelphia. Daniel Ernest Johnson, Jr., became the Archdeacon for Colored Work of the Diocese of Arkansas in 1914. E.L. Braithwaite became Georgia's first Archdeacon for Colored Work in 1918.

Some of the early archdeacons were white, but increasingly bishops turned to black clergy to exercise the function. With their leadership, the loss of black membership halted and the number of black parishioners began to increase. The majority of black Episcopal congregations that exist today began under the leadership of the archdeacons during the years 1890 to 1920.

By the second decade of the twentieth century, some Episcopalians began to ask why the blacks could not serve as bishops as well. After all, the Archdeacons for Colored Work were already performing most of the administrative functions of bishops in relationship to black congregations. This was the question that bishops and deputies brought to the General Convention of 1916.

Yet at that time many white parishioners would have been hesitant to accept the authority of black bishops. Indeed, given the national mood during the years of World War I—when the U.S. government was adopting a national policy of segregation—it was amazing that the topic was discussed at all.

Members of the General Convention approached the question from two directions. Some favored the creation of separate, nongeographical dioceses with their own "racial"—i.e., black—bishops. A second group believed that the adoption of canons for suffragan bishops—assistant bishops without the right of succession—at the 1910 General Convention offered a better solution.

The suffragan party won. North Carolina and Arkansas were the first dioceses to take advantage of the provision. In 1918 they respectively consecrated Henry B. Delaney (1858-1928) and Edward T. Demby (1869-1957) as suffragan bishops.

The decision was a step in the direction of greater equality, but it was only a partial step. Black bishops represented the Episcopal Church in the community and exercised authority over black congregations. It would not be until 1970, however, that a black person was elected to lead all the people of an American diocese. In that year, John Burgess was elected the bishop of Massachusetts.

Those interested in the racial and ethnic character of American denominations might want to read Wade Roof and William McKinney's American Mainline Religion: Its Changing Shape of the Religious Establishment *(New Brunswick: Rutgers University Press, 1987).*

Disappearing Balconies

Avid mystery fans may recall the role of the balcony in Dorothy Sayer's *Nine Tailors*. Sayer's hero, Lord Peter Wimsey, hunts for a necklace that has been stolen and hidden by a dishonest butler. On the basis of a rhyme written by the butler for one of his confederates, Lord Peter determines that the jewels are hidden in the local church. Searching the interior of the building, he spots a logical but unreachable location. Yet he is undaunted. He asks the Anglican vicar whether the building once had a balcony. The vicar notes that it had a balcony at the time of the robbery but indicates that the balcony has since been removed. Wimsey secures a ladder and locates the jewels.

Wimsey's guess—that a balcony had been removed—was a logical one for the 1920s. At that time, balconies were rapidly disappearing from Anglican churches. Where they remained, they were declining in importance. Had Wimsey's investigations been set in an Episcopal Church in the United States, he would have discovered the same phenomenon. The number of American balconies also decreased following World War I.

Balconies were to American Episcopalians of the 1920s a symbol of an outdated social and economic system. Episcopalians a hundred years before had adopted a pew rental system to finance their parishes: Members of the congregations made annual pledges to the church and were given assigned seating; those who were unable or unwilling to pay this rent were consigned to balconies. There were some advantages to the system. It allowed the parish, for example, to make a clear distinction between operating costs and missionary outreach; pew rent supported the parish expenses, and a series of designated offerings throughout the year funded missionary endeavors. These advantages were, however, outweighed by serious disadvantages: people in the balconies, who were in some cases required to use separate outside entrances, felt removed from the life of the parish. They often were practically "excommunicated," unable to come forward to receive the elements when the eucharist was celebrated. Moreover, the pew holders were dwindling in number, and their ability to support the operating costs of the parish was questionable.

Innovative congregations in large cities began experimenting with free seating in the mid-nineteenth century. For the majority of Episcopal congregations, however, it would not be until the conclusion of World War I that the pew rent system finally died.

Buoyed with enthusiasm by the victory in Europe, American Christians believed that, if properly organized, they could do anything. A nationwide Interchurch World Movement set out to raise one billion dollars for missionary work. Within the Episcopal Church, the General Convention planned an All Nation Canvass in order to enlist everyone in Episcopal congregations—those who sat in balconies and those who held pews—in supporting an expanded church program. The canvass proved more successful than pew rents in raising funds; pledge envelopes rapidly replaced pew rents as the normative source of parish income.

With the abandonment of the pew rental system, balconies were soon deserted. Architects, renovating churches in the surge of liturgical interest that accompanied the adoption of the 1928 *Book of Common Prayer*, removed many of them. Where they remained in place, most were left empty.

Much Beloved Daughter

Bishop Ronald Owen Hall faced a serious problem. His missionary diocese, the Anglican Diocese of Victoria-Hong Kong, had always had a shortage of priests. But in 1944 the situation was particularly critical. With Hong Kong behind Japanese lines, there was no hope of recruiting additional missionary clergy from England. The Japanese occupation also limited overseas financial support. Without that, it was difficult to keep the diocese's training college open. The school lacked a president and was poorly equipped to prepare additional candidates for ordination. A growing population in the diocese made the problem yet more difficult. The 1941 *Crockford's Clerical Directory* reported approximately 5,700 church members in the diocese. The 1947 edition would estimate that church membership had risen to 20,000.

The bishop had vacancies in at least nine of his relatively small number of parishes. In some cases a priest was able to serve several parishes in the same city, but elsewhere not even this was possible. In the whole of Macao, a populous island near Hong Kong, there was not a single priest. The Japanese compounded the problem by refusing permission for priests from Hong Kong to visit the island.

The bishop did, however, have one deaconess at work on Macao. Frances Li Tim Oi (b. 1907), whom he had ordained in 1941, served the Anglican congregations on the island. She proved herself a faithful pastor in the difficult years of Japanese occupation. By 1943 the bishop began to wonder whether ordaining her to the priesthood would not be the most responsible course of action for him to take. She had proven pastoral abilities. She had both the intellectual gifts and the educational experience for which he looked in a candidate for priesthood. The daughter of a former school principal, who had herself served as a school head, she was a 1940 graduate of the Canton Union Theological College. Many male Chinese clergy had graduated from the same institution.

As he grew more fixed in his conviction that ordination was the right course, Bishop Hall wrote to then Archbishop of Canterbury William Temple. When 1944 opened without a reply from the archbishop, Hall decided to take action. On January 25, 1944, he ordained Deaconess Li to the priesthood. She served Anglicans on Macao for the remainder of the war. When the war ended, she moved to a congregation in Canton.

The war years were difficult for Li; the later 1940s would, however, prove more difficult still. She faced two challenges in rapid succession. The first came from the church hierarchy. The bishops at the 1948 Lambeth Conference discussed Li's ordination to the priesthood. Despite a supporting resolution from Li's diocese and favorable recommendations from two bishops of other Chinese dioceses, Lambeth adopted a strongly negative resolution calling Li's ordination a "radical" step that "transgressed against" Anglican tradition and order. The Lambeth Conference was an advisory body with no formal jurisdiction over provinces of the Anglican Church. The attitude of the assembled bishops was so negative, however, that Li and her bishop accepted the judgment of the body as if it had jurisdiction. She stopped exercising priestly functions. The bishop ordained no more deaconesses to the priesthood.

The second challenge came from the new government that took control of the Chinese mainland in the year following the Lambeth Conference. Mao Tse-tung's communist government allowed some religious self-expression but rejected any non-Chinese influence on Chinese churches. The old Anglican Diocese of Victoria divided into two dioceses, one within communist China and the other limited to independent Hong Kong and Macao. Remaining in Canton, Li was cut off from many of her fellow Anglicans. The lack of outside support and a governmental policy designed to discourage separate denominations led to the closing of Li's congregation in 1952. Li accepted the government policy and in time became a professor at the Canton Union Theological College. Yet even acceptance of the policy did not bring security. The Cultural Revolutionaries of the later years of Mao's rule closed the seminary and banned public worship. They sent her to work in a factory.

Li's fortunes began to improve in the 1970's, however. The decade opened with the decision of the Diocese of Hong Kong and Macao to begin again to ordain women to the priesthood. In Advent of 1971, Bishop Gilbert Baker ordained Jane Hwang Hsien Yuen and Joyce Bennett as the second and third female Anglican priests. By 1977 Canada, the United States, and New Zealand had all followed the

Chinese lead. In 1979 a more liberal communist Chinese government allowed the churches of Canton to reopen, and Li resumed her active ministry.

In January of 1984, Li traveled to London for a festival celebration of the fortieth anniversary of her ordination to the priesthood. Large crowds gathered at Westminster Abbey to see the patient Chinese priest who had been prevented from exercising her priesthood for three decades.

Li's autobiography, Much Beloved Daughter, *is available from Morehouse Publishing.*

The Death and Burial of Canon XV

In the year that he died, the Reverend Odell Greenleaf Harris (1903-83) completed an autobiography. He titled it *It Can Be Done*, but the subtitle he chose was perhaps more indicative of his subject matter: "The autobiography of a Black Priest of the Protestant Episcopal Church who started under the bottom and moved to the top."

Harris was born in a rural North Carolina community that had no schools of any kind for black children. Yet by moving several times and balancing a series of jobs, he was able to complete college (St. Augustine's and Virginia State College) and seminary (Bishop Payne Divinity School). After ordination, he served the church in a succession of positions in the dioceses of North Carolina, Virginia, Southern Virginia, and Georgia.

Harris told his story with feeling and with a sense of accomplishment. There was much that he had done in his life. Yet as he looked back on his ordained ministry there was one thing of which he was especially proud. It was, to use his words, "the death and burial of Canon XV."

Canon XV was the provision in the church law of the Diocese of Southern Virginia that allowed for partial segregation of blacks. Most Southern dioceses and some dioceses outside the South had similar provisions. Such canons established "Colored Convocations." Each black congregation sent lay delegates and its clergy to the convocation. The convocation, in turn, sent a fixed number of delegates to the diocesan convention. In 1940 in southern Virginia, for example, all black clergy were allowed to participate in diocesan council, but the Colored Convocation was permitted to choose only two black laypersons to attend; each white parish, in contrast, was entitled to lay representation at diocesan council.

From 1937 to 1949 Harris served on the faculty of Bishop Payne Divinity School in Petersburg, Virginia. During the same period he was active in the Diocese of Southern Virginia, serving as the dean of the Colored Convocation (1943-47) and archdeacon (1949-51). He campaigned tirelessly for an end to segregation in the diocese. In 1944, he and other black Episcopalians were able to convince the diocesan council to increase the number of lay representatives from the Colored Convocation from two to six. In 1946, they were able to convince the council to allow the congregations of Colored Convocation representation at council on the same basis as white parishes. The year 1946 was also when Harris argued successfully on the diocese's executive board for the raising of salaries of black mission clergy to the level given white mission clergy. In 1947, black clerical and lay delegates staged a walkout during lunch at diocesan council in order to protest the separate seating with which they were provided during meals; the tactic proved effective, and seating at meals at future councils was desegregated.

Yet Canon VX remained in the canons. For Harris it was a continual reminder of the secondary status of black Episcopalians. White parishes were divided into geographical regions, each of which had its own convocation. Black parishes, regardless of location, were part of the Colored Convocation.

With a larger black representation at council as a result of changes in representation adopted in 1944 and 1946, Harris felt the time had come to ask for the repeal of Canon XV. At the fifty-sixth Annual Council of the Diocese of Southern Virginia that took place in May of 1948, he proposed abolition of the Colored Convocation. Anxious to see how his fellow council members voted, he called for a show of hands, rather than the usual voice vote. The vote carried. As Harris would later write in his autobiography, "This, then killed Canon XV and all allied supports for segregation in the Diocese of Southern Virginia. This canon had been in effect since 1890. It can be done."

In 1949 the Diocese of Virginia followed the lead of Southern Virginia and abolished its own Colored Convocation. In the same year, Bishop Payne Divinity School stopped accepting students. Virginia Seminary, which accepted its first black student in 1951, officially merged with Payne in 1953.

Odell Greenleaf Harris's It Can Be Done *is available from Virginia Seminary Book Service, Seminary Post Office, Alexandria, VA 22304 (703-370-6161).*

Graduation Time in the 1940s

In many ways the graduation ceremonies at Philadelphia Divinity School and at Bishop Payne Divinity School in Petersburg, Virginia, in the 1940s were like any Episcopal seminary graduations. Students and their assembled families and friends listened to oratory of church dignitaries and waited for the presentation of degrees. They gave thanks for their years of study and awaited anxiously for the beginning of their professional careers.

Yet in one way the graduations at Philadelphia and Bishop Payne in the 1940s were unlike any that had ever taken place in Episcopal seminaries. For in the forties, Philadelphia and Bishop Payne were in the midst of a bold experiment. From 1945 to 1949 Bishop Payne, and from 1939 to 1951 Philadelphia, accepted female students in special Christian education programs.

The women who completed the programs were the first female graduates of any of the Episcopal seminaries. Prior to 1939 the Episcopal Church had only provided for the education of female church workers in separate female institutions. The first of these was the Bishop Potter Memorial House in Philadelphia, which, between 1867 and 1891, trained women in nursing, Christian education, and missions. Other institutions followed. The New York Training School for Deaconesses (New York City, 1890), St. Phoebe's Church Training House (San Francisco, 1891), the Church Training and Deaconess School of the Diocese of Pennsylvania (Philadelphia, 1891), and the Deaconess Training School of the Pacific (Berkeley, 1908) all prepared women to serve as deaconesses. Windham House (New York City, 1928) prepared women for roles in Christian education. In 1942 the School of Christian Service and Deaconess Training School changed its name to St. Margaret's House and adopted a similar emphasis on Christian education. Bishop Tuttle Training School (Raleigh, 1925) trained black women for church work.

Episcopal men studied in separate institutions—theological seminaries of which the oldest dated to the 1820s. The faculties of these theological seminaries were composed entirely of men until the opening of World War II. At that time, however, the shortage of available men and the proven track record of women in Christian education combined to convince the administrations of Episcopal seminaries to begin to add female faculty members. Adelaide Case became the Professor of Religious Education at the Episcopal Theological School (Cambridge, Massachusetts) in 1941. Katharine Arnett Grammer became a resident tutor in Christian Education at Philadelphia in 1943. In 1945 the administration of Bishop Payne Divinity School hired Martha Pray as the Instructor in Christian Education. Four years later Marion Kelleran came to Virginia Seminary as the Adjunct Professor of Christian Education.

As members of the Woman's Auxiliary to the Board of Missions (later renamed the Episcopal Churchwomen), began to point out, if women could teach at theological seminaries, it might be appropriate for them to study there as well. Philadelphia led the way, designating the Church Training and Deaconess School as its women's department in 1939. In 1945 Bishop Payne followed suit, admitting its first four female students. With only three men completing their studies at Payne in 1947, females composed half of the graduating class.

Unfortunately, the Christian education program for women at Payne, and at Philadelphia did not survive long after the close of the 1940s. The women's program at Philadelphia was discontinued in 1952, as the institution reorganized to accommodate an increasing number of returning veterans. That at Payne, which had an all-black student body, was a casualty of desegregation. Payne stopped admitting students in 1949 and merged with Virginia Seminary in 1953. The combined institution admitted both black and white males, but the program for women was abandoned.

After approximately ten years, other Episcopal seminaries began to follow the lead of Philadelphia and of Bishop Payne. The Church Divinity School of the Pacific's graduating class of 1955 included Jane Buchanan, and the class of 1957 included Marianne H. Micks and Muriel James. The three were the first women to receive a three-year degree from an Episcopal seminary. The Episcopal Theological School and Virginia enrolled female students in 1958. Yet it was the women at Philadelphia and Bishop Payne who had been first. Their classes pointed the way toward decades of change that would follow. By 1987, female students composed 42 percent of the combined student bodies of all Episcopal seminaries.

The Post-World War II Clergy Boom

In 1952 the Joint Standing Commission on Theological Education submitted a report to the General Convention. Committee members themselves had suggested to the previous Convention the need for the report. An important change was taking place in the Episcopal Church's theological seminaries; they felt that members of the General Convention needed to be informed about it.

The ten major seminaries (Berkeley in New Haven, Bexley in Ohio, the Church Divinity School of the Pacific in California, the Episcopal Theological School in Massachusetts, General Seminary in New York, Nashotah House in Wisconsin, Philadelphia Divinity School, Seabury-Western in Chicago, the School of Theology of the University of the South in Sewanee, and Virginia) had faced declining enrollments throughout the 1930s and early 1940s. Now, as the commission report would indicate, they had moved from famine to feast. They had already begun to experience a swelling enrollment in 1948-49. By 1952, the growth in numbers was even more evident. The commission report summed up this situation in a few brief sentences:

> It is obvious that the state of the Seminaries can change and has changed very rapidly, so that judgment upon their operations must be constantly revised. The number of students reported in 1947-48, for example, was 508, and the capacity of the ten schools given in the 1949 Journal was 750-800. Yet in 1950-51 their enrollment soared to 1,043. . . . (*Journal of the General Convention* 1952, p. 642)

The seminaries were overflowing.

This postwar boom in seminary attendance would have both short-term and long-term effects on the church. In order to respond in the short run, seminary administrations were forced to launch ambitious building programs and to expand the size of their faculties. Virginia, for example, built five new dormitories and doubled the size of its faculty in the 1950s. In addition, an eleventh seminary opened, the Episcopal Theological Seminary of the Southwest in Austin. It was the first new Episcopal seminary since the nineteenth century.

As the students graduated, they were able to provide an adequate supply of clergy for parishes that had previously been unable to secure full-time clergy. In addition, the Episcopal Church was growing rapidly in the expanding suburbs; new graduates were able to serve in many new congregations. The growth in the number of clergy and congregations in the 1950s contributed to a sense of optimism and excitement in the church.

The increased supply of clergy also subtly changed the church. In its entire history, the Episcopal Church in America had never had an adequate supply of clergy. From the colonial era on, congregations outnumbered clergy. On any given Sunday, priests would preside over a portion of Episcopal worship services, with lay readers and deaconesses presiding over the others. This situation was rapidly changing, however. In 1957 the church had more clergy than parishes for the first time in its history.

Much of the course of the church in the 1960s and 1970s was made possible or necessary by this new availability of clergy. Here are three important examples:

1. The liturgical revival that had culminated in the adoption of the 1979 *Book of Common Prayer* was based on the premise that the Sunday eucharist was the normative service of the church. Such celebrations were only possible because of the increased availability of clergy.

2. The new clergy of the postwar seminary boom filled many roles that had previously been filled by laypersons. This increasingly clerical leadership produced a backlash—a revival of interest in lay ministry in the 1970s and 1980s.

3. Since the revival of the female diaconate in the middle of the nineteenth century, deaconesses had served many of the smaller congregations that were unattractive to male priests. With the general growth in the church and the availability of male clergy, there were decreasing numbers of such congregations in which deaconesses might serve. With a decline in the female permanent diaconate, female Episcopalians began to search for other avenues of leadership. In 1976 the General Convention approved the ordination of women to the priesthood.

David Sumner's The Episcopal Church's History 1945-1985 *details many of the changes in the Episcopal Church since World War II. It is available from Morehouse Publishing.*

Suggestions for Further Reading

Many of the preceding chapters conclude with bibliographical notes. I would suggest, as an additional source of information, several journals and newsletters that are useful to those interested in the history of the Episcopal Church. They carry shorter articles about the church and generally include reviews of current books.

The Historical Society of the Episcopal Church (P.O. Box 2247, Austin, TX 78705) publishes *Anglican and Episcopal History* four times a year. In addition to articles and reviews, the magazine now also carries "church reviews"—descriptive pieces on the history and character of specific Episcopal congregations. The Institute of Early American History and Culture (P.O. Box 220, Williamsburg, VA 23187), publishes *The William and Mary Quarterly,* which often includes articles on the colonial Anglican Church. The Women's History Project (c/o General Theological Seminary, 175 Ninth Avenue, New York, NY 10011) issues a quarterly newsletter that focuses on the role that women have played in the Episcopal Church. The *Historiographer* is a regular publication for diocesan and parish archivists, which often carries announcements of recent parish histories. It is sent to those who join the National Episcopal Historians Association (Box 1507, Lucerne Valley, CA 92356).

Index

Allen, Richard   53-54
Ayres, Anne   90-93
Bacon, Lady Anne   21-22
Bilney, Thomas   9-12, 15
Bishop Payne Divinity School   123-126
Black, Mary   93
Book Annexed   111-112
Book of Common Prayer   1, 10, 19, 21, 36, 40, 42, 110, 112
Book of Offices   112
Bray, Thomas   38-39, 108
Breck, James Lloyd   81
Brent, Charles Henry   109
Buchanan, Jane   126
Burgess, John   117
Burnham, Mary   104
Case, Adelaide   126
Celtic Christianity   4-6
Chase, Philander   74-75
Chicago-Lambeth Quadrilateral   107-109
Church of Scotland   35-37
Cranmer, Thomas   10, 12, 16-19, 35
Crummell, Alexander   54, 82-83
Cyprian of Carthage   1-3
Dare, Virginia   27-28
Deaconesses   70, 78-79, 89-93, 104, 128
Delaney, Henry B.   116
Demby, Edward T.   116
desegregation   123-124
Edward VI   12, 18-19, 21, 23-24, 26, 35-36
Elizabeth I   12, 18-19, 24, 26, 35-36
Enmegahbowh   96, 97
Episcopal colleges   60-62, 75
Fliedner, Frederica and Theodore   78-79, 92
Free African Society   53-54
Gantt, Edward, Jr.   49-52

Gardiner, Allen   63-64
Gallaudet, Thomas   86-88
Grammer, Katharine Arnett   126
Griswold, Alexander Viets   77
Hakluyt, Richard   30
Harriot, Thomas   27-28
Harris, Odell Greenleaf   123-124
Henry VIII   7-8, 12, 18, 35
Hobart, John Henry   58-59, 108
Homilies, the Book of   18-20, 26
Hooker, Richard   23-24, 25
Hopkins, John Henry   1-2, 98-99
Hunt, Robert   29-31
Huntington, William Reed   107-109, 111
Jamestown   27, 29, 31
Jewel, John   2-3, 21-22, 35
Jones, Absalom   53-54
Kaiserswerth   78-79, 89
Kelleran, Marion   126
Kemper, Jackson   80-81
Key, Francis Scott   103
Latimer, Hugh   12, 35
Li Tim Oi, Frances   120-122
Luther, Martin   7-9, 11-12
McIlvaine, Charles Pettit   100-102
Mahan, Milo   94-95
Manteo   28
Mary I   19, 21, 24, 35
Mayhew, Jonathan   45-46
Meade, William   71-73, 84-85
Minard, Catherine   93
Moor, Thoroughgood   40-41
More, Thomas   7-8
Moore, Richard Channing   72, 76-77
Muhlenberg, William Augustus   67-68, 89-90, 91
Neve, Frederick William   113-114
Nonjurors   43
Oakerhater, David Pendleton   104
Otey, James Hervey   74-75
Pendleton, Alice   103-104
Perkins, William   25-26
pew rents   118-119
Plazas, Carlos   61
Pray, Martha   126
Proposed Book   110
"Racial" Bishops and Archdeacons   115-117

Reichardt, Gertrude   79
revivalism   76-77
Roanoke Island   27-28
Rowson, Susanna Haswell   65-66
SAMS   64
SPCK   39
SPG   39, 42
Seabury, Samuel   42, 44, 49-51, 57-58
Smith, Benjamin Bosworth   74
Smith, William   50
Soule, Ida   106
Stringfellow, Horace   92-93
Syle, Henry Winter   87
Talbot, John   42-44
Temple, Charlotte   65-66
Twing, Mary Abbot   105-106
United Thank Offering   105-106
vestries   32-34
Wainwright, Jonathan Mayhew   46
Weems, Mason Locke   50-52, 55-56
Welton, Robert   43-44
Whipple, Henry Benjamin   96-97
White, William   54, 57, 67, 68, 70
White Horse Inn   10, 11-13, 15
Williams, Peter Jr.   54, 82
Wilmer, William Holland   72-73, 100
Wolsey, Thomas   8, 14-15
women's ordination to priesthood   69-70, 120-122, 128